ALSO FROM UK DRI'

Teaching a Learner Driver –
A guide for Amateur Instructors
Learning to Drive –
The Learner Driver's Manual
The Learner Driver's Logbook –
Lesson Plan & Progress Record
The Driving Test & How to Pass –
An Examiner's Guide to the 'L' Test

The Highway Code
How to Drive on a Motorway
Driving at Night & in Bad Weather

250 THEORY TEST QUESTIONS FOR:

Cars - Motorcycles - LGV - PCV - ADI

HIGHWAY CODE PLUS THEORY TEST QUESTIONS FOR:

Cars - Motorcycles - LGV - PCV - ADI

All available from www.ukdrivingskills.co.uk

250 THEORY TEST QUESTIONS FOR CARS

UK Driving Skills
Theory Test Question Series

Don L. Gates

www.ukdrivingskills.co.uk

Revised: 31/10/22

250 THEORY TEST QUESTIONS FOR CARS

This product includes the Driver and Vehicle Standards Agency (DVSA) revision question bank.

The Driver and Vehicle Standards Agency (DVSA) has given permission for the reproduction of Crown copyright material. DVSA does not accept responsibility for the accuracy of the reproduction.

Contents

About the Theory Test

In order to take a theory test, you must have lived in England, Wales or Scotland for at least 185 days in the last 12 months before the day you sit your test. You need to obtain a provisional driving licence before booking a test.

You must pass your theory test before you can take a practical driving test.

What to Take With You

You must take your UK photo card driving licence to your test. If you have a licence from Northern Ireland, take the photo card and paper counterpart licence. Your test will be cancelled and you will lose your fee if you do not take the correct things with you.

If you have an old style paper licence you must also take a valid passport for photo ID. If you do not have a passport, you need to get a photo card licence.

You will need to show your licence or ID to the staff when you arrive at the test centre. There will also be security checks to make sure that you're not carrying anything which could enable you to contact anyone outside of the test centre.

If you have any personal possessions, these must be placed in a secure locker. It's best to take nothing with you that you don't really need.

Starting the Test

A member of staff will take you to a room where other candidates will be sat in cubicles also taking the test. You must be quiet but don't be afraid to ask questions.

The test is fairly straightforward and all the instructions will be shown on the screen in front of you. If you wish you can choose to have a 15 minute practise session to get used to the way the test works.

Multiple Choice Questions

Once you begin the test, you will have 57 minutes to answer 50 questions. Three of these will be based on a short video clip. You need to score at least 43 points to pass.

In addition to this book, you can also use our online theory test practise pages to make sure that you're ready to pass at -
https://www.ukdrivingskills.co.uk/theory-test-practise/

Hazard Perception

You may take a 3 minute break if you wish before starting the second part of the test. When you're ready, you should put on the provided headphones to watch an explanatory video of the hazard perception element.

You will be shown 14 video clips during which you need to click the mouse when you see a 'developing hazard', such as a vehicle about to emerge from a junction or a pedestrian about to step off the kerb; something which would cause you as a driver to alter speed or direction.

Click at the right time to score a maximum of 5 points for each clip. Don't just click randomly as you may be penalised for clicking too many times. One of the clips will have 2 hazards for you to identify. There is a maximum of 75 points and you need a minimum of 44 points to pass.

2

Test Result

You will get your test result shortly after finishing. You need to reach the minimum score in both parts to pass.

If you're not successful you must wait at least 3 working days before you can try again. If you pass, you will need to use your pass certificate number in order to go ahead and book your practical driving test. The certificate is valid for 2 years. If you haven't passed your driving test within this time you will need to sit the theory test again.

Book a Theory Test

When you're ready to take a theory test, you can either:

- call the central booking line on 0300 200 11 22
- use the online booking system at - https://www.gov.uk/book-theory-test (easiest)

Before booking make sure that you have your:

- UK driving licence number
- an email address
- credit or debit card for payment

The current cost for cars & motorcycles is £23

Special Needs

If you have any special needs you must mention this at the time of booking. Where possible, the theory test centre may be able to make adjustments to help you overcome any difficulties you may have.

About this Book

The material in this book is reproduced under licence from the Driver & Vehicle Standards Agency.

Questions are based on the official DVSA theory test question revision bank. They are designed to help you revise and practise for your theory test.

Questions marked with an asterisk* are not from the DVSA question bank and are © Copyright UK Driving Skills

Whilst every care is taken to ensure the accuracy of these questions and answers, if you do spot any errors please contact UK Driving Skills via our website to bring these to our attention.

Theory Test Questions for Cars

Each practise set consists of 50 multiple choice questions. Mark the letter to the left of each answer you think is correct.

You will find the correct answers over the page; you will also be given an explanation of the answer helping to reinforce your knowledge on the subject.

Test One

Question 1

You are keeping well back while waiting to overtake a large vehicle. What should you do if a car moves into the gap ahead of you?

A   Sound your horn

B   Drop further back

C   Stay close to the other car

D   Overtake both vehicles

Question 2

What does this sign mean?

A   Two-way traffic crossing a one-way road

B   Oncoming traffic has priority

C   Two-way traffic ahead

D   Contraflow system ahead

Answers

Question 1

B - Sometimes your separation distance is shortened by a driver moving into the gap you've allowed. When this happens, react positively, stay calm and drop further back to re-establish a safe following distance.

Question 2

C - This sign may be at the end of a dual carriageway or a one-way street. It's there to warn you of oncoming traffic.

Question 3 *

As you are driving along, you see a long vehicle starting to emerge from a junction on your right. The driver is about to swing into your path. What should you do?

A   Reduce speed and allow the driver to emerge

B   Maintain your speed as you have right of way

C   Warn the driver by flashing your lights

D   Mount the pavement to avoid it

Question 4

A group of horse riders comes towards you. What should you do if the leading rider's horse becomes nervous of your presence?

A   Increase speed to pass the riders quickly

B   Continue driving carefully and keep well to the left

C   Brake to a stop as quickly as possible

D   Brake gently to a stop until they have passed

Question 5

What should you do if you see a large box fall from a lorry onto the motorway?

A   Go to the next emergency telephone and report the hazard

B   Catch up with the lorry and try to get the driver's attention

C   Stop near to the box until the police arrive

D   Pull over to the hard shoulder, then remove the box

Answers

Question 3

A - Drivers of long vehicles sometimes need to swing wide so that their trailers don't cut in across the pavement, and they won't be able to pull out and clear the junction as quickly as a car driver would. To be safe, you need to slow down and give the driver time.

Question 4

D - If any animal you pass on the road becomes unsettled, you should brake gently to avoid startling them and come to a stop. A nervous animal is unpredictable, so you should wait until it has settled or passed by.

Question 5

A - Lorry drivers can be unaware of objects falling from their vehicles. If you see something fall onto a motorway, look to see if the driver pulls over. If they don't stop, don't attempt to retrieve the object yourself. Pull onto the hard shoulder near an emergency telephone and report the hazard.

Question 6 *

What would help you get into the correct lane in good time?

A   Areas of hatched markings

B   Double white lines along the road

C   Warning signs along the road

D   Place names painted on the road

Question 7

How can you reduce the environmental harm caused by your motor vehicle?

A   Only use it for short journeys

B   Don't service it so often

C   Avoid driving too slowly

D   Reduce the amount of acceleration

Answers

Question 6

D - The names of towns and cities may be painted on the road at busy junctions and complex road systems. Their purpose is to let you move into the correct lane in good time, allowing traffic to flow more freely.

Question 7

D - Engines that burn fossil fuels produce exhaust emissions that are harmful to health. The harder you make the engine work, the more emissions it will produce. Engines also use more fuel and produce higher levels of emissions when they're cold. Anything you can do to reduce your use of fossil fuels will help the environment.

Question 8

What is the main hazard shown in this scene?

A Vehicles turning right

B Vehicles doing a U-turn

C The cyclist waiting on the grass

D Parked cars around the corner

Question 9 *

Anti-lock brakes are designed to help prevent you from skidding. When is this likely to be least effective?

A When it is foggy

B When the weather is cold

C When the road surface is loose

D When the tarmac is fresh

Answers

Question 8

C - Look at the picture carefully and try to imagine you're there. The cyclist in this picture appears to be trying to cross the road. You must be able to deal with the unexpected, especially when you're approaching a hazardous junction. Look well ahead to give yourself time to deal with any hazards.

Question 9

C - There will be little for your tyres to grip onto when the road surface is loose or damaged. In this situation anti-lock braking may not be of much help.

Question 10

You park at night on a road with a 40 mph speed limit. What should you do?

A   Park facing the traffic

B   Leave parking lights on

C   Leave dipped headlights on

D   Park near a street light

Question 11 *

On a motorway with three lanes, which lane should you normally use when you are driving at 70 mph?

A   The left hand lane

B   The centre lane

C   The right hand lane

D   The lane which has least traffic

Question 12

What can a loose filler cap on your diesel fuel tank cause?

A   It can make the engine difficult to start

B   It can make the roads slippery for other road users

C   It can increase your vehicle's fuel consumption

D   It can increase the level of exhaust emissions

Answers

Question 10

B - You must use parking lights when parking at night on a road or in a lay-by on a road with a speed limit greater than 30 mph. You must also park in the direction of the traffic flow and not close to a junction.

Question 11

A - Regardless of how many lanes a motorway has, the left hand lane is always the one you should normally use except when overtaking.

Question 12

B - Diesel fuel can spill out if your filler cap isn't secured properly. This is most likely to occur on bends, junctions and roundabouts, where it will make the road slippery, especially if it's wet. At the end of a dry spell of weather, the road surfaces may have a high level of diesel spillage that hasn't been washed away by rain.

Question 13

A single carriageway road has this sign. What's the maximum permitted speed for a car towing a trailer?

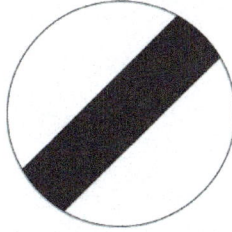

A 30 mph

B 40 mph

C 50 mph

D 60 mph

Question 14 *

What would you expect to find when you see this sign?

A A steep uphill gradient

B A steep downhill gradient

C A sharp bend to the right

D An area of chevrons painted on the road

Answers

Question 13

C - When you're towing a trailer, a reduced speed limit also applies on dual carriageways and motorways. These lower speed limits apply to vehicles pulling all sorts of trailers, including caravans and horse boxes.

Question 14

C - Black and white chevron signs warn of a sharp deviation or bend in your road. You should slow down on approach and make sure that you are travelling at a safe speed before entering the corner.

Question 15 *

You see a pedestrian approaching a zebra crossing. What should you normally do?

A   Accelerate before they step onto the crossing

B   Slow down and allow them to cross if they want to

C   Ignore them as they are still on the pavement

D   Stop and wave at them to cross the road

Question 16

Which of these should you do when driving in fog?

A   Use sidelights only to reduce dazzle

B   Switch on main beam headlights

C   Allow more time for your journey

D   Keep the vehicle ahead in sight

Answers

Question 15

B - Pedestrians have right of way once they step onto the crossing, but you should always slow down and be ready to stop to allow them to step out. Never wave them on, they could step into another danger they have not seen.

Question 16

C - Don't venture out if your journey isn't necessary. If you have to travel and someone is expecting you at the other end, let them know that you'll be taking longer than usual for your journey. This will stop them worrying if you don't turn up on time and will also take the pressure off you, so you don't feel you have to rush.

Question 17

What should you do when going through a contraflow system on a motorway?

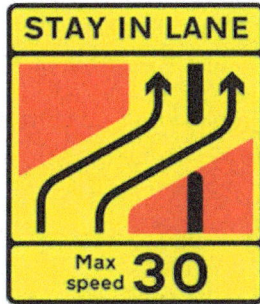

A   Ensure that you keep to 30 mph

B   Keep a good distance from the vehicle ahead

C   Switch lanes to keep the traffic flowing

D   Stay close to the vehicle ahead to reduce queues

Question 18 *

You see some elderly and slow moving people starting to cross the road ahead of you. What should you do?

A   Wave them to continue so they know it is safe

B   Slow down and give them time to cross

C   Go wide and drive around them

D   Warn them of your approach by tapping the horn

Answers

Question 17

B - At roadworks, and especially where a contraflow system is operating, a speed restriction is likely to be in place. Keep to the lower speed limit and don't

- switch lanes
- get too close to the vehicle in front of you.

Be aware that there will be no permanent barrier between you and the oncoming traffic.

Question 18

B - Elderly people may have impaired judgement, they may not realise what speed you are doing, and they may be slow to cross the road. You need to be patient and considerate. You should never wave people to cross, they may step into a danger that you haven't seen.

Question 19 *

Windscreens have pillars which can partially restrict your view. When is this most likely to be a problem?

A   When there is oncoming traffic

B   When you are driving at higher speeds

C   When someone is following you

D   When you are turning at a junction

Question 20

You're towing a caravan. Which is the safest type of rear-view mirror to use?

A   Interior wide-angle mirror

B   Extended-arm side mirrors

C   Ordinary door mirrors

D   Ordinary interior mirror

Question 21

When should you inflate your tyres to more than their normal pressure?

A   When the roads are slippery

B   When the vehicle is fitted with anti-lock brakes

C   When the tyre tread is worn below 2 mm

D   When carrying a heavy load

Answers

Question 19

D - When approaching bends and junctions, you need to look to the sides to widen your view across the bend, and to look for others before emerging. It is when turning your head that the door pillars may obstruct your view. Move your head to look past them!

Question 20

B - Towing a large trailer or caravan can greatly reduce your view of the road behind. You may need to fit extended-arm side mirrors so that you can see clearly behind and down both sides of the caravan or trailer.

Question 21

D - Check the vehicle handbook. This should give you guidance on the correct tyre pressures for your vehicle and when you may need to adjust them. If you're carrying a heavy load, you may need to adjust the headlights as well. Most cars have a switch on the dashboard to do this.

Question 22

What does the white line along the side of the road indicate?

A   The edge of the carriageway

B   The approach to a hazard

C   No parking

D   No overtaking

Question 23 *

A driver emerges from a junction ahead of you. You have to brake to avoid them. What should you do next?

A   Pull back and keep your distance

B   Follow closely to make them aware of your presence

C   Warn them with a flash of your lights

D   Overtake them immediately

Answers

Question 22

A - A continuous white line is used on many roads to indicate the edge of the carriageway. This can be useful when visibility is restricted. The line is discontinued at junctions, lay-bys, and entrances to or exits from private drives.

Question 23

A - There are many inconsiderate drivers on our roads, or the driver may be new and lacking in judgement. It's not easy, but if you can remain calm and ignore the error, you will remain a better and more focussed driver.

Question 24

What can happen if your car's wheels are unbalanced?

A   The steering will pull to one side

B   The steering wheel will vibrate

C   The brakes will be less effective

D   The steering will become heavy

Question 25

You are turning left into a side road. What hazard should you be especially aware of?

A   A change in speed limit

B   Pedestrians

C   Traffic congestion

D   Parked vehicles

Question 26

In which conditions will your overall stopping distance increase?

A   In the rain

B   In fog

C   At night

D   In strong winds

Answers

Question 24

B - If your wheels are out of balance, it will cause the steering to vibrate at certain speeds. This isn't a fault that will put itself right, so take your vehicle to a garage or tyre fitter to have the wheels rebalanced.

Question 25

B - Make sure that you've reduced your speed and are in the correct gear for the turn. Look into the road before you turn and always give way to any pedestrians who are crossing.

Question 26

A - Extra care should be taken in wet weather. On wet roads, your stopping distance could be double that in dry conditions.

Question 27

What does this sign mean?

A   Give way to oncoming vehicles

B   Approaching traffic passes you on both sides

C   Turn off at the next available junction

D   Pass on either side

Question 28

On which occasion may you enter a box junction?

A   When there are fewer than two vehicles ahead

B   When signalled by another road user

C   When your exit road is clear

D   When traffic signs direct you

Answers

Question 27

D - These signs are seen in one-way streets that have more than one lane. When you see this sign, use the route that's the most convenient and doesn't require a late change of direction.

Question 28

C - Yellow box junctions are marked on the road to prevent the road becoming blocked. Don't enter the box unless your exit road is clear. You may wait in the box if you want to turn right and your exit road is clear but oncoming traffic or other vehicles waiting to turn right are preventing you from making the turn.

Question 29

Your vehicle has a puncture on a motorway. What should you do?

A Drive slowly to the next service area to get assistance

B Pull up on the hard shoulder. Change the wheel as quickly as possible

C Pull up on the hard shoulder. Use the emergency phone to get assistance

D Switch on your hazard warning lights. Stop in your lane

Question 30

You are on a motorway. There is a contraflow system ahead. What would you expect to find?

A Temporary traffic lights

B Lower speed limits

C Wider lanes than normal

D Speed humps

Answers

Question 29

C - Pull up on the hard shoulder and make your way to the nearest emergency telephone to call for assistance. Don't attempt to repair your vehicle while it's on the hard shoulder, because of the risk posed by traffic passing at high speeds.

Question 30

B - When approaching a contraflow system, reduce speed in good time and obey all speed limits. You may be travelling in a narrower lane than normal, with no permanent barrier between you and the oncoming traffic. Be aware that the hard shoulder may be used for traffic and the road ahead could be obstructed by slow-moving or broken-down vehicles.

Question 31

What must you do at this junction?

A   Stop behind the line, then edge forward to see clearly

B   Stop beyond the line, at a point where you can see clearly

C   Stop only if there is traffic on the main road

D   Stop only if you are turning to the left

Question 32

You're on a motorway at night. In which situation may you have your headlights switched off?

A   When there are vehicles close in front of you

B   When you are travelling below 50 mph

C   When the motorway is brightly lit

D   When your vehicle is broken down on the hard shoulder

Answers

Question 31

A - The 'stop' sign has been put here because the view into the main road is poor. You must stop because it won't be possible to take proper observation while you're moving.

Question 32

D - Always use your headlights at night on a motorway, unless you've had to stop on the hard shoulder. If you have to use the hard shoulder, switch off your headlights but leave your parking lights on, so that your vehicle can be seen by other road users.

Question 33

Unless signs show otherwise, what's the national speed limit for a car or motorcycle on a motorway?

A   50 mph

B   60 mph

C   70 mph

D   80 mph

Question 34 *

What should you do if a driver coming up behind dazzles you with their lights at night?

A   Use the anti-dazzle position for your mirror

B   Avoid using your mirrors at night

C   Brake regularly to flash your brake lights

D   Switch on your main beam headlights

Answers

Question 33

C - The national speed limit for a car or motorcycle on a motorway is 70 mph. Lower speed limits may be in force; for example, at roadworks. Variable speed limits also operate in some areas when the motorway is very busy. Cars or motorcycles towing trailers are subject to a lower speed limit.

Question 34

A - Rear view mirrors have a small clip on the bottom edge, which will tilt the mirror and prevent you from being dazzled. You can click this back when the problem has gone away. Some modern cars now have automatically dipping mirrors.

Question 35

What might you expect to happen in this situation?

A   Traffic will move into the right-hand lane

B   Traffic speed will increase

C   Traffic will move into the left-hand lane

D   Traffic won't need to change position

Question 36

On a road where trams operate, which of these vehicles will be most at risk from the tram rails?

A   Cars

B   Cycles

C   Buses

D   Lorries

Answers

Question 35

C - The right-hand lane is about to close. Be courteous and allow the traffic to merge into the left-hand lane.

Question 36

B - The narrow wheels of a bicycle can become stuck in the tram rails, causing the cyclist to stop suddenly, wobble or even lose balance altogether. The tram lines are also slippery, which could cause a cyclist to slide or fall off. Make sure that you allow riders plenty of room in these situations.

Question 37

What information is found on a vehicle registration document?

A   The registered keeper

B   The type of insurance cover

C   The service history details

D   The date of the MOT

Question 38 *

How does a toucan crossing differ from other types of crossing?

A   Horse riders can also use it

B   Traffic wardens control it

C   It only operates at peak times

D   Cyclists can also use it

Question 39

Where can you find reflective amber studs on a motorway?

A   Separating the slip road from the motorway

B   On the left-hand edge of the road

C   On the right-hand edge of the road

D   Separating the lanes

Answers

Question 37

A - Every vehicle used on the road has a registration document. This shows the vehicle's details, including date of first registration, registration number, registered keeper, previous keeper, make of vehicle, engine size, chassis number, year of manufacture and colour.

Question 38

D - Toucan crossings are shared by pedestrians and cyclists, who are permitted to cycle across. The signals are push-button-operated and there's no flashing amber phase.

Question 39

C - At night or in poor visibility, reflective studs on the road help you to judge your position on the carriageway. Amber studs mark the edge of the central reservation.

Question 40

On a motorway, when should the hard shoulder be used?

A   When answering a mobile phone

B   When an emergency arises

C   When taking a short rest

D   When checking a road map

Question 41

Why must you take extra care when turning right at this junction?

A   The road surface is poor

B   The footpaths are narrow

C   The road markings are faint

D   The view is restricted

Answers

Question 40

B - The hard shoulder should only be used in a genuine emergency. If possible, and if it's safe, use a roadside telephone to call for help. This will give your exact location to the operator. Never cross the carriageway or a slip road to use a telephone on the other side of the road.

Question 41

D - You may have to pull forward slowly until you can see up and down the road. Be aware that the traffic approaching the junction can't see you either. If you don't know that it's clear, don't go.

Question 42

When will you feel the effects of engine braking?

A   When you only use the handbrake

B   When you are in neutral

C   When you change to a lower gear

D   When you change to a higher gear

Question 43

You are driving on a wet road. You have to stop your vehicle in an emergency to avoid a pedestrian. What should you do?

A   Apply both the handbrake and footbrake

B   Keep both hands on the steering wheel

C   Change quickly down the gears

D   Make sure there is nothing behind you

Question 44

What is the legal minimum depth of tread for car tyres?

A   1.6 mm

B   2.5 mm

C   4 mm

D   1 mm

Answers

Question 42

C - When you take your foot off the accelerator, engines have a natural resistance to turn, caused mainly by the cylinder compression. Changing to a lower gear requires the engine to turn faster and so it will have greater resistance than when it's made to turn more slowly. When going downhill, changing to a lower gear will therefore help to keep the vehicle's speed in check.

Question 43

B - As you drive, look well ahead and all around so that you're ready for any hazards that might develop. If you have to stop in an emergency, react as soon as you can while keeping control of the vehicle. Keep both hands on the steering wheel so you can control the vehicle's direction of travel.

Question 44

A - Car tyres must have sufficient depth of tread to give them a good grip on the road surface. The legal minimum for cars is 1.6 mm. This depth should be across the central three-quarters of the breadth of the tyre and around the entire circumference.

Question 45 *

MOT tests include an exhaust emission test. Why is this carried out?

A   To help protect the environment

B   To measure your fuel consumption

C   To check the engine's power output

D   To check which fuel you are using

Question 46 *

What does it mean when the amber light flashes after you have stopped at a pelican crossing?

A   You must wait for pedestrians to clear the crossing

B   You now have right of way over the pedestrians

C   You must still wait for people to step out

D   You must wait for the green light before moving off

Question 47

You want to turn right from a junction but your view is restricted by parked vehicles. What should you do?

A   Move out quickly, but be prepared to stop

B   Sound your horn and pull out if there is no reply

C   Stop, then move slowly forward until you have a clear view

D   Stop, get out and look along the main road to check

Answers

Question 45

A - Emission tests are carried out to make sure your vehicle's engine is operating efficiently. This ensures the pollution produced by the engine is kept to a minimum. If your vehicle isn't serviced regularly, it may fail the annual MOT test.

Question 46

A - Any pedestrians still on the road must be allowed to finish crossing, but anyone on the footpath should not now begin to cross. You may drive on as soon as it is safe to do so. You don't need to wait for the green light.

Question 47

C - If you want to turn right from a junction and your view is restricted, stop. Ease forward until you can see – something might be approaching. If you don't know, don't go.

Question 48

You're driving behind a large goods vehicle. The driver signals left but starts moving out to the right. What should you do?

A   Slow down and wait for the driver to turn

B   Assume that the driver has given the wrong signal

C   Take down the vehicle number to report the driver

D   Prepare to pass the vehicle on its left

Question 49

You are driving in traffic at the speed limit for the road. What should you do if the driver behind is trying to overtake?

A   Move closer to the car ahead, so the driver behind has no room to overtake

B   Wave the driver behind to overtake when it's safe

C   Keep a steady course and allow the driver behind to overtake

D   Accelerate to get away from the other driver

Question 50 *

When does the law state that you MUST stop your vehicle?

A   When you have been involved in an accident

B   Before turning right at a major crossroads

C   When a member of the public waves you down

D   When you get an amber warning light on your dashboard

Answers

Question 48

A - Large, long vehicles need extra room when making turns at junctions. They may move out to the right in order to make a left turn. Keep well back and don't attempt to pass them on their left.

Question 49

C - Keep a steady course to give the driver behind an opportunity to overtake safely. If necessary, slow down. Reacting incorrectly to another driver's impatience can lead to danger.

Question 50

A - The law requires you to stop if you have been involved in an accident. You must exchange details with anyone else involved before continuing.

2022

The Highway Code

The Rules of the Road

UK Driving Skills
www.ukdrivingskills.co.uk

49

Test Two

Question 1

You are coming up to a roundabout. A cyclist on your left is signalling to turn right. What should you do?

A   Overtake wide on the right

B   Give a warning with your horn

C   Signal the cyclist to move across

D   Stay behind the cyclist

Question 2

What's the main benefit of driving a four-wheel-drive vehicle?

A   Improved grip on the road

B   Lower fuel consumption

C   Shorter stopping distances

D   Improved passenger comfort

Question 3 *

When following another vehicle, why should you not follow it too closely?

A   There will be too much turbulence

B   Your engine will be starved of air

C   Your view will be restricted

D   Your sat nav may lose its signal

Answers

Question 1

D - If you're following a cyclist who's signalling to turn right at a roundabout, stay behind and leave plenty of room.

Although it may not be considered safe by many, the Highway Code states that cyclists may turn right using the left-hand lane; you need to be aware that the rider may cross your path as you approach your exit.

Question 2

A - By driving all four wheels, the vehicle has maximum grip on the road. This grip is especially helpful when travelling on slippery or uneven surfaces. However, having four-wheel drive doesn't replace the skills you need to drive safely.

Question 3

C - The closer you get the rear of another vehicle the less you will be able to see past it. This will limit your ability to react in time to hazards.

Question 4

You're on a three-lane motorway. A red cross is showing above the hard shoulder and mandatory speed limits above all other lanes. What does this mean?

A   The hard shoulder can be used as a rest area if you feel tired

B   The hard shoulder is for emergency or breakdown use only

C   The hard shoulder can be used as a normal running lane

D   The hard shoulder has no speed limit

Question 5 *

When is it against the law to sound your vehicle's horn in a built up area?

A   At any time when you're stationary

B   At any time during the night

C   Between 11.30 pm and 7.00 am

D   Between midnight and 8 am

Answers

Question 4

B - A red cross above the hard shoulder shows that it's closed as a running lane and should only be used for emergencies or breakdowns. On a smart motorway, the hard shoulder may be used as a running lane at busy times. This will be shown by a mandatory speed limit on the gantry above the hard shoulder.

Question 5

C - You mustn't sound your horn in a built-up area between 11.30 pm and 7.00 am in order to avoid disturbing people who may be sleeping. When stationary, although you may sound your horn to warn someone else of danger, it should not be used in any other situation when stationary even during the day.

Question 6

When are anti-lock brakes (ABS) most effective?

A   When you keep pumping the foot brake to prevent skidding

B   When you brake normally but grip the steering wheel tightly

C   When you brake promptly and firmly until you have stopped

D   When you apply the handbrake to reduce the stopping distance

Question 7

You are driving along this road. The driver on the left is reversing from a driveway. What should you do?

A   Move to the opposite side of the road

B   Drive through as you have priority

C   Speed up and drive through quickly

D   Sound your horn and be prepared to stop

Answers

Question 6

C - If you have ABS and need to stop in an emergency, keep your foot firmly on the brake pedal until the vehicle has stopped. When the ABS operates, you may hear a grating sound and feel vibration through the brake pedal. This is normal and you should maintain pressure on the brake pedal until the vehicle stops.

Question 7

D - White lights at the rear of a car show that the driver has selected reverse gear. Sound your horn to warn the other driver of your presence, and reduce your speed as a precaution.

Question 8

Traffic signs giving orders are generally which shape?

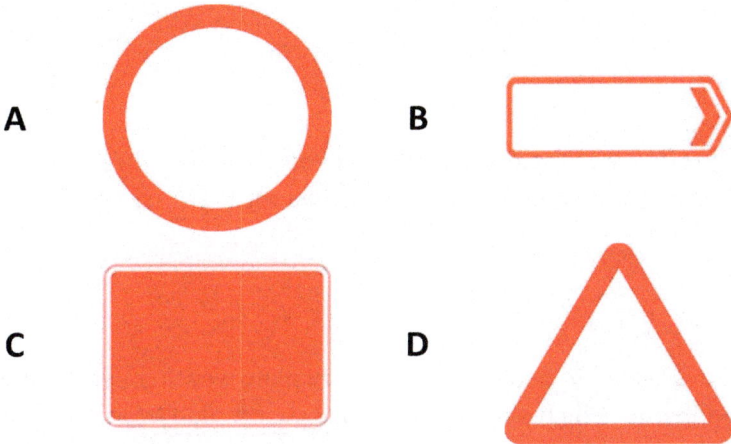

A

B

C

D

Question 9

You're driving in windy conditions on the motorway. What action should you take when overtaking large vehicles?

A   Drive closer to them than normal

B   Be prepared for a sudden gust of wind

C   Stay alongside until you're sure they have seen you

D   Straddle the lanes while you are passing

Answers

Question 8

A - Road signs in the shape of a circle give orders. Those with a red circle are mostly prohibitive. Signs giving orders must always be obeyed.

Question 9

B - Motorways are open and exposed to prevailing weather conditions. In windy conditions, a high-sided vehicle may shelter you from the wind as you pass. As you emerge past it, you may suddenly be buffeted by the wind.

Question 10 *

What should you do when moving off from behind a parked car on the left?

A   Keep looking your left hand shoulder

B   Use mirrors and glance to your right

C   Signal before putting the car into gear

D   Edge out so that someone stops for you

Question 11

You wish to turn right ahead. Why should you take up the correct position in good time?

A   To help other road users know what you intend to do

B   To allow other drivers to pull out in front of you

C   To give a better view into the road that you are joining

D   To make your steering easier to manage

Question 12 *

You have an old vehicle battery which is no longer of any use. What should you do with it?

A   Leave it outside for someone to collect

B   Take it to a local recycling centre

C   Bag it securely before putting in the waste bin

D   Place it in a recycling bin

Answers

Question 10

B - Before moving off, you should use both the interior and exterior mirrors to check that the road is clear. Glance to your right to cover the blind spots and, if necessary, give a signal to warn other road users of your intentions but be careful not to mislead others with a poorly timed signal.

Question 11

A - If you wish to turn right into a side road, take up your position in good time. Move to the centre of the road when it's safe to do so. This will allow vehicles to pass you on the left. Early planning will show other traffic what you intend to do.

Question 12

B - Batteries contain corrosive acid which can damage the environment. They should be taken to an official recycling site for safe disposal.

Question 13

What should you do when you leave your car unattended for a few minutes?

A   Leave the engine running

B   Switch the engine off but leave the key in

C   Leave a note in the window

D   Lock it and remove the key

Question 14

You think the driver of the vehicle in front has forgotten to cancel their right indicator. What should you do?

A   Flash your lights to alert the driver

B   Turn your right indicator on and off

C   Overtake on the left if there is room

D   Stay behind and don't overtake

Question 15

You are carrying an 11-year-old child in the back seat of your car. They are under 1.35 metres (4 feet 5 inches) tall. What must you make sure of?

A   That they sit between two belted people

B   That they can fasten their own seat belt

C   That a suitable child restraint is available

D   That they can see clearly out of the front window

Answers

Question 13

D - Always switch off the engine, remove the key and lock your car, even if you're only leaving it for a few minutes.

Question 14

D - Be cautious and don't attempt to overtake. The driver may be unsure of the location of a junction and may turn suddenly. Flashing your lights or using your own indicator is a signal that could easily be misinterpreted by anyone who sees it.

Question 15

C - As the driver, it's your responsibility to make sure that children are secure and safe in your vehicle. Make yourself familiar with the rules. In a few very exceptional cases when a child restraint isn't available, an adult seat belt must be used.

Question 16

At an incident, someone is suffering from severe burns. What should you do to help them?

A   Apply moisturiser to the injuries

B   Wrap the burns in bandages

C   Remove anything sticking to the burns

D   Douse the burns with cool water

Question 17

You have just passed your practical test. You don't hold a full licence in another category. Within two years you get six penalty points on your licence. What will you have to do?

A   Retake only your theory test

B   Retake your theory and practical tests

C   Retake only your practical test

D   Reapply for your full licence immediately

Question 18

You are travelling along a motorway and feel tired. Where should you stop to rest?

A   On the hard shoulder

B   At the nearest service area

C   On a slip road

D   On the central reservation

Answers

Question 16

D - Your priority is to cool the burns with clean, cool water. Its coolness will help take the heat out of the burns and relieve the pain. Keep the wound doused for at least 10 minutes if possible.

Question 17

B - If you accumulate six or more penalty points within two years of gaining your first full licence, it will be revoked. The six or more points include any gained due to offences you committed before passing your test. If this happens, you may only drive as a learner until you pass both the theory and practical tests again.

Question 18

B - If you feel tired, stop at the nearest service area. If that's too far away, leave the motorway at the next exit and find a safe place to stop. You mustn't stop on the carriageway or hard shoulder of a motorway except in an emergency, when in a traffic queue, or when signalled to do so by a police officer, a traffic officer or traffic signals. Plan your journey so that you have regular rest stops.

Question 19 *

Why would you change into a lower gear after passing this sign?

A   To control your speed using engine braking

B   To provide extra acceleration

C   To give better fuel economy

D   To get more power for the climb

Question 20

What should you do if a trailer starts to swing from side to side while you're towing it?

A   Let go of the steering wheel and let it correct itself

B   Steer in the direction the trailer is swinging

C   Accelerate gradually until it stabilises

D   Ease off the accelerator to reduce your speed

Answers

Question 19

A - This sign gives you an early warning that the road ahead will slope downhill. Prepare to alter your speed and gear. Looking at the sign from left to right will show you whether the road slopes uphill or downhill.

Question 20

D - Strong winds or buffeting from large vehicles can cause a trailer or caravan to swing from side to side ('snake'). If this happens, ease off the accelerator. Don't brake harshly, steer sharply or increase your speed.

Question 21

Which instrument-panel warning light would show that headlights are on full beam?

A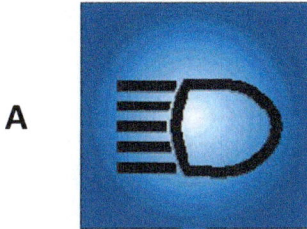

B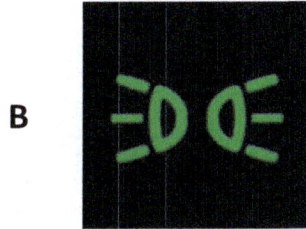

C

D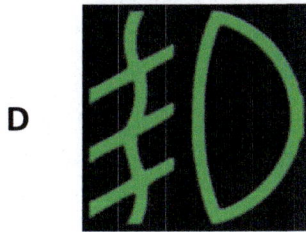

Question 22

How would you identify a section of road used by trams?

A   There would be a different surface texture

B   There would be metal studs around it

C   There would be zigzag markings alongside it

D   There would be yellow hatch markings around it

Answers

Question 21

A - You should be aware of all the warning lights and visual aids on the vehicle you're driving. If you're driving a vehicle for the first time, you should familiarise yourself with all the controls, warning lights and visual aids before you set off.

Question 22

A - Trams may run on roads used by other vehicles and pedestrians. The section of road used by trams is known as the reserved area and should be kept clear. It usually has a different surface, edged with white lane markings.

Question 23

What does this traffic sign mean?

A   Hump bridge

B   Humps in the road

C   Steep camber

D   Soft verges

Question 24

You are approaching a red traffic light. What will the signal show next?

A   Red and amber

B   Green alone

C   Amber alone

D   Green and amber

Answers

Question 23

B - These humps have been put in place to slow the traffic down. They're usually found in residential areas. Slow down to an appropriate speed.

Question 24

A - Red amber will show next, this is still a stop signal. If you know the light sequence, you can plan your approach accordingly. Adjusting your speed correctly will help you to drive more smoothly and also to safe fuel.

Question 25

You are looking for somewhere to park your vehicle. The area is full except for spaces marked 'disabled use'. What can you do?

A   You can use these spaces when elsewhere is full

B   You can park in one of these spaces if you stay with your vehicle

C   You can use one of the spaces as long as one is kept free

D   You can't park there, unless you are permitted to do so

Question 26 *

What does this red cross on a blue background mean?

A   No waiting

B   No stopping

C   No entry

D   No vehicles

Answers

Question 25

D - It's illegal to park in a space reserved for disabled users unless you're permitted to do so. These spaces are provided for people with limited mobility, who may need extra space to get in and out of their vehicle.

Question 26

B - The sign indicates that the road is a 'clearway' where no stopping is allowed. There may also be an information plate telling you what times this restriction is in force. If there is no time plate, you should assume that the clearway is in operation 24 hours.

Question 27 *

You want to turn left from a main road into a side road. What should you do on the approach to it?

A   Stay in a wide position to give yourself room

B   Keep as close to the kerb as possible

C   Swing out to the right just before turning

D   Keep well to the left on the main road

Question 28 *

What does this arrow marking in the middle of the road mean?

A   Traffic should use the hard shoulder

B   The road is about to bend to the left

C   Overtaking drivers should move back to the left

D   It is a safe place to overtake

Answers

Question 27

D - You should position well to the left but not so close to the kerb that you are in danger of mounting it as you turn. You should never swing out before turning, this could endanger traffic which may be passing on your right.

Question 28

C - The white arrow warns any overtaking drivers that they should move back to the left. There is probably a hazard ahead such as a dip in the road, a bend, or a traffic island.

Question 29

You take some cough medicine given to you by a friend. What should you do before driving?

A   Ask your friend if taking the medicine affected their driving

B   Drink some strong coffee one hour before driving

C   Check the label to see if the medicine will affect your driving

D   Drive a short distance to see if the medicine is affecting you

Question 30

What is the right-hand lane used for on a three-lane motorway?

A   Emergency vehicles only

B   Overtaking

C   Vehicles towing trailers

D   Coaches only

Question 31

What colour are the reflective studs between a motorway and its slip road?

A   Amber

B   White

C   Green

D   Red

Answers

Question 29

C - If you've taken medicine, never drive without first checking what the side effects might be; they might affect your judgement and perception, and therefore endanger lives.

Question 30

B - You should keep to the left and only use the right-hand lane if you're passing slower-moving traffic. Once you have overtaken be ready to return to the middle or left-hand lane as soon as it's safe and practical to do so.

Question 31

C - The studs between the carriageway and the hard shoulder are normally red. These change to green where there's a slip road, helping you to identify slip roads when visibility is poor or when it's dark.

Question 32 *

It's a windy day. You're about to pass a cyclist. Why do you need to be particularly careful?

A   The wind speed could suddenly change

B   The rider may not be able to keep a steady course

C   The rider may not be able to maintain normal speed

D   The wind might make them go faster than normal

Question 33

You are following a slower-moving vehicle. There is a junction just ahead on the right. What should you do?

A   Overtake after checking your mirrors and signalling

B   Only consider overtaking when you are past the junction

C   Accelerate quickly to pass before the junction

D   Slow down and prepare to overtake on the left

Answers

Question 32

B - In windy conditions riders can easily be blown off course. There is a danger that they could be blown across in front of you; especially when they're passing places such as gaps in buildings where they're suddenly exposed to a gust of wind. You need to make allowances for this by giving them as much room as you can before overtaking.

Question 33

B - You should never overtake as you approach a junction. If a vehicle emerged from the junction while you were overtaking, a dangerous situation could develop very quickly.

Question 34

What should you do when approaching traffic lights where red and amber are showing together?

A   Drive on if the way is clear

B   Start to edge over the stop line

C   Wait for the green light

D   Start to pick up speed

Question 35

You are the first to arrive at the scene of a serious incident. What should you do?

A   Leave as soon as another motorist arrives

B   Flag down other motorists to help you

C   Drag all casualties away from the vehicles

D   Call the emergency services promptly

Answers

Question 34

C - You should not cross the line until the green light shows. Where the lights have just changed, be aware that other traffic may still be crossing and always look to make sure that your way is clear.

Question 35

D - At a crash scene you can help in practical ways, even if you aren't trained in first aid. Call the emergency services and make sure you don't put yourself or anyone else in danger. The safest way to warn other traffic is by switching on your hazard warning lights.

Question 36

What should you do if your anti-lock brake (ABS) warning light stays on?

A   Check the brake-fluid level

B   Check the footbrake free play

C   Make sure this is corrected at your next service

D   Have the brakes checked as soon as possible

Question 37

What does this traffic sign mean?

A   Ring road

B   Mini-roundabout

C   No vehicles

D   Roundabout

Answers

Question 36

D - Consult the vehicle handbook or a garage before driving the vehicle any further. Only drive to a garage if it's safe to do so. If you aren't sure, get expert help.

Question 37

D - As you approach a roundabout, look well ahead and check all signs. Decide which exit you wish to take and move into the correct position as you approach the roundabout, signalling as required.

Question 38 *

You've been following a slow-moving motorcyclist for quite some time. What should you do if you're unsure what the rider is going to do?

A   Go quickly past on their left

B   Go quickly past on their right

C   Tap the horn before carefully overtaking

D   Stay behind them and keep your distance

Question 39

You're driving towards this left-hand bend. What danger should you be most aware of?

A   A change in speed limit

B   No white lines in the centre of the road

C   No sign to warn you of the bend

D   Pedestrians walking towards you

Answers

Question 38

C - Initially you should stay behind and keep your distance, but there may come a point when they are causing a problem for you and following traffic. You need to make them aware of your presence with a light tap on the horn. If they continue to ride at very low speed then you may then cautiously overtake if it's safe.

Question 39

D - Pedestrians walking on a road with no pavement should walk against the direction of the traffic. You can't see around this bend: there may be hidden dangers. Always keep this in mind and give yourself time to react if a hazard does appear.

Question 40 *

You're about to go on a long journey. You've been involved in an argument that has made you feel angry. What should you do?

A   Make sure the argument is settled before you leave

B   Play some loud music to let off steam

C   Drive around local roads to begin with

D   Take time to calm down before you set off

Question 41

What does the law require you to keep in good condition?

A   Seat belt

B   Gears

C   Transmission

D   Door locks

Answers

Question 40

D - If you're feeling upset or angry, you'll find it much more difficult to concentrate on your driving. You should wait until you've calmed down before starting a journey.

Question 41

A - Unless exempt, you and your passengers must wear a seat belt (or suitable child restraint). The seat belts in your car must be in good condition and working properly; they'll be checked during its MOT test.

Question 42

What does this sign mean?

A   End of two-way road

B   Give priority to vehicles coming towards you

C   You have priority over vehicles coming towards you

D   Start of two-way road

Question 43 *

Why should you use dipped headlights at night, even when the area is well lit?

A   You will save on battery power

B   You will be able to maintain a higher speed

C   Because the law requires you to do so

D   Other people will be able to see you more easily

Answers

Question 42

C - You may have priority but don't force your way through. Show courtesy and consideration to other road users. Even though you have priority, make sure oncoming traffic is going to give way before you continue.

Question 43

D - In a well lit area, although sidelights may be the legal minimum requirement; using dipped headlights will not only increase your view of the road ahead, but it will also make sure that others can see you.

Question 44

You wish to tow a trailer. Where would you find the maximum nose-weight allowed on your vehicle's tow hitch?

A   In the vehicle handbook

B   In The Highway Code

C   In your vehicle registration certificate

D   In your licence documents

Question 45

You are driving on an open road in dry weather. What should the minimum distance be between you and the vehicle in front?

A   A two-second time gap

B   One car length

C   Two metres (6 feet 6 inches)

D   Two car lengths

Question 46

How can you use your vehicle's engine to control your speed?

A   By changing to a lower gear

B   By selecting reverse gear

C   By changing to a higher gear

D   By selecting neutral

Answers

Question 44

A - You must know how to load your trailer or caravan so that the hitch exerts an appropriate downward force on the tow ball. Information about the maximum permitted nose-weight can be found in your vehicle handbook or obtained from your vehicle manufacturer's agent.

Question 45

A - One way of checking there's a safe distance between you and the vehicle in front is to use the two-second rule. To check for a two-second time gap, choose a stationary object ahead, such as a bridge or road sign. When the car in front passes the object, say 'Only a fool breaks the two-second rule'. If you reach the object before you finish saying the phrase, you're too close and need to increase the gap.

Question 46

A - You should brake and slow down before selecting a lower gear. The gear can then be used to keep the speed low and help you control the vehicle. This is particularly helpful on long downhill stretches, where brake fade can occur if the brakes overheat.

Question 47

Is it necessary to give a signal when you're passing parked vehicles?

A   It's only necessary when there's traffic behind

B   It's only necessary when there's oncoming traffic

C   It might not be necessary

D   It's always necessary

Question 48

You are approaching a red light at a puffin crossing. Pedestrians are on the crossing. When will the red light change?

A   When you start to edge forward onto the crossing

B   When the pedestrians have cleared the crossing

C   When the pedestrians push the button on the other side

D   When a driver from the opposite direction reaches the crossing

Question 49

Why should you test your brakes after driving through a ford?

A   To check your brake lights are working

B   To make sure you can stop safely

C   To bleed air from the brake system

D   To remove the water from your tyres

Answers

Question 47

C - A signal might not be necessary where there's no-one to benefit from it, or where the signal could confuse other road users. Forward planning and taking an early and steady course will remove the need to routinely signal to pass parked vehicles or obstructions.

Question 48

B - A sensor will automatically detect that the pedestrians have reached a safe position. Don't drive on until the green light shows and it's safe for you to do so.

Question 49

B - At a ford, the road passes through a stream at a place where the water is normally shallow. When you've gone through the water, you should test your brakes and if necessary dry them out. To do this, first check that you won't cause danger to traffic behind. Then apply a light brake pressure while moving slowly. Make sure your brakes are working properly before resuming normal driving.

Question 50 *

What should you do when you see an emergency vehicle behind you?

A   Move aside and slow down when it is safe

B   Continue normally and let them decide when to pass

C   Maintain your speed but signal left to let them know they can pass

D   Brake to an immediate stop until they pass

Answers

Question 50

A - You should do what you can to let the emergency vehicle pass, but do not suddenly stop as this could take others by surprise and cause danger in itself. Reduce speed and move over to the left as soon as it is safe to do so.

Learning to Drive

The Learner Driver's Manual

LP UK Driving Skills

Test Three

Question 1

Where would you expect to see these red and yellow markers?

A   On a motorway sign

B   On a railway bridge

C   On a large goods vehicle

D   On a diversion sign

Question 2

A casualty isn't breathing normally and needs CPR. At what rate should you press down and release on the centre of their chest?

A   10 per minute

B   120 per minute

C   60 per minute

D   240 per minute

Answers

Question 1

C - These markers must be fitted to vehicles over 13 metres long, large goods vehicles, and rubbish skips placed in the road. They're reflective to make them easier to see in the dark.

Question 2

B - If a casualty isn't breathing normally, cardiopulmonary resuscitation (CPR) may be needed to maintain circulation. Place two hands on the centre of the chest and press down hard and fast – around 5–6 centimetres and about twice a second.

Question 3

You are travelling along a motorway. When are you allowed to overtake on the left?

A   If you're within one mile of your exit

B   If the driver ahead won't move over to let you pass

C   If you're in stationary traffic but the hard shoulder is clear

D   If you're driving in a slow-moving traffic queue

Question 4 *

After servicing your own car, what should you do with the old oil?

A   Take it to an official disposal and recycling site

B   Mix it with some detergent before pouring it into the drain

C   Pour it into the soil and top with sand

D   Put it into a bottle and place in your recycle bin

Question 5

What should you do if you park on the road when it's foggy?

A   Leave dipped headlights and fog lights switched on

B   Leave dipped headlights switched on

C   Leave sidelights switched on

D   Leave main-beam headlights switched on

Answers

Question 3

D - Never overtake on the left, unless the traffic is moving in queues and the queue on your right is moving more slowly than the one you're in. Don't be tempted to keep changing lanes to join a faster queue; you'll find they all slow down and speed up at various intervals.

Question 4

A - Engine oil is full of toxins and pollutants which should only be disposed of safely by taking it to an official recycling site.

Question 5

C - If you have to park your vehicle in foggy conditions, try to find a place to park off the road. If this isn't possible, park on the road facing in the same direction as the traffic. Leave your sidelights switched on and make sure they're clean.

Question 6

What's the meaning of this sign?

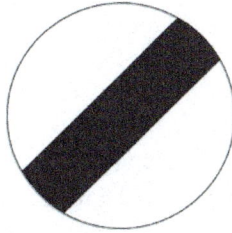

A   National speed limit applies

B   Local speed limit applies

C   No entry for vehicles

D   No waiting on the carriageway

Question 7

Other drivers may sometimes flash their headlights at you. In which situation are they allowed to do this?

A   To warn of a radar speed trap ahead

B   To show that they are giving way to you

C   To warn you of their presence

D   To let you know there is a fault with your vehicle

Answers

Question 6

A - This sign doesn't tell you the speed limit in figures. You should know the speed limit for the type of road that you're on and the type of vehicle that you're driving. Study your copy of The Highway Code.

Question 7

C - If other drivers flash their headlights, this isn't a signal to show priority. The flashing of headlights has the same meaning as sounding the horn: it's a warning of their presence. Always be very wary in this situation and make sure that you know what the other person intends and that it is safe for whatever you intend to do.

Question 8 *

You want to reverse park a car between two vehicles on the side of the road. As a guide, what would be the minimum size for a suitable parking space?

A   Three car lengths

B   One and a half car lengths

C   Two car lengths

D   Two and a half car lengths

Question 9

Trams can move both quietly and quickly. What other feature of trams should you be especially aware of?

A   They can't steer to avoid you

B   They don't have a horn

C   They can't stop for cars

D   They don't have lights

Question 10

You are about to drive home but you can't find the glasses you need to wear. What should you do?

A   Drive home slowly, keeping to quiet roads

B   Borrow a friend's glasses and use those

C   Drive home at night, so that the lights will help you

D   Find a way of getting home without driving

Answers

Question 8

B - Reverse or parallel parking between parked vehicles is an essential skill to master. How large the space needs to be depends on the driver's skill and the size of your car.

Question 9

A - Electric trams run on rails and can't steer to avoid you. Keep a lookout for trams in areas where they operate, as they move very quietly and you might not hear them approaching.

Question 10

D - If you need to wear glasses for driving, it's illegal to drive without them. You must be able to see clearly when you're driving.

Question 11 *

You're about to move from the right-hand lane of a motorway back into the centre lane after overtaking. Why should you consider signalling left before doing so?

A   Because it's always necessary to signal left after overtaking

B   In case drivers in the left-hand lane are about to move out

C   In case drivers ahead are about to leave the motorway

D   To let the driver you have passed know that you are moving in

Question 12

You break down on a motorway. You need to call for help. Why may it be better to use an emergency roadside telephone rather than a mobile phone?

A   It connects you to a local garage

B   Using a mobile phone will distract other drivers

C   It allows easy location by the emergency services

D   Mobile phones don't work on motorways

Answers

Question 11

B - Moving back to the left after overtaking is what you're supposed to do, and what other drivers expect you to do. It should not normally need a signal to overstate the obvious. On a road with three lanes however, as you're about to move back to the middle lane, drivers in the left could also be thinking about moving into that lane to overtake vehicles ahead of them. It is these drivers who may need a signal from you.

Question 12

C - On a motorway, it's best to use a roadside emergency telephone so that the emergency services are able to find you easily. The location of the nearest telephone is shown by an arrow on marker posts at the edge of the hard shoulder. If you use a mobile, the operator will need to know your exact location. Before you call, find out the number on the nearest marker post. This number will identify your exact location.

Question 13 *

Where would you see this sign?

A   At the end of a dual carriageway

B   At the beginning of a contra-flow system

C   At the end of a one-way street

D   At a road narrowing

Question 14 *

What does this sign mean?

A   Dual-carriageway ends

B   Merging traffic on both sides

C   There is a fork in the road

D   Road narrows both sides

Answers

Question 13

D - This sign will be used where the road narrows, often as a result of traffic calming measures. When you see this you should give way to oncoming traffic.

Question 14

D - The road is about to narrow on both sides, you need to be more aware of any overtaking or oncoming traffic.

Question 15 *

Following a long spell of hot dry weather, it's now starting to rain. What do you need to be aware of?

A   There may be an increased risk of skidding

B   The cleaner road surface will give a better grip

C   Braking distances will be shortened

D   The road surface may start to break up

Question 16

What does the term 'blind spot' mean?

A   An area not visible to the driver

B   An area covered by your right-hand mirror

C   An area not covered by your headlights

D   An area covered by your left-hand mirror

Answers

Question 15

A - When it stays dry for some time, deposits such as oil and rubber can build up on the road surface. When rain then falls onto this mixture it can result in a very slippery surface until it's washed away. You should make allowances for this when braking and cornering as the risk of skidding can be much greater.

Question 16

A - Modern vehicles provide the driver with a good view of both the road ahead and behind using well-positioned mirrors. However, the mirrors can't see every angle of the scene behind and to the sides of the vehicle. This is why it's essential that you know when and how to check your blind spots, so that you're aware of any hidden hazards.

Question 17

What does this traffic sign mean?

A No parking

B No road markings

C No through road

D No entry

Question 18 *

Why should you not follow a large goods vehicle too closely?

A The driver may not be able to see you

B It will hold up your progress

C It will cause you to use more fuel

D You may not be able to see it signalling

Answers

Question 17

D - 'No entry' signs are used in places such as one-way streets to prevent vehicles driving against the traffic. To ignore one would be dangerous, both for yourself and for other road users, as well as being against the law.

Question 18

A - Drivers of large and long vehicles may not be able to see you in their mirrors if you get too close to their rear. If you cannot see their mirrors, then they probably cannot see you and may not realise that you are there.

Question 19

You arrive at an incident. There is no danger from fire or further collisions. What is your first priority when attending to an unconscious motorcyclist?

A   Check whether they are breathing normally

B   Check whether they are bleeding

C   Check whether they have any broken bones

D   Check whether their helmet can be removed

Question 20

What is an effect of drinking alcohol?

A   A loss of confidence

B   Faster reactions

C   Greater awareness of danger

D   Poor judgement of speed

Question 21

You are about to emerge from a junction. Your passenger tells you it is clear. When should you rely on their judgement?

A   Never; you should always look for yourself

B   When the roads are very busy

C   When the roads are very quiet

D   Only when they are a qualified driver

Answers

Question 19

A - At the scene of an incident, always be aware of danger from further collisions or fire. The first priority when dealing with an unconscious person is to ensure they're breathing normally. If they're having difficulty breathing, follow the DR ABC code.

Question 20

D - Alcohol will severely reduce your ability to drive or ride safely and there are serious consequences if you're caught over the drink-drive limit. It's known that alcohol can

- affect your judgement
- cause overconfidence
- reduce coordination and control.

Question 21

A - Your passenger may be inexperienced in judging traffic situations, may have a poor view or may not have seen a potential hazard. You're responsible for your own safety and that of your passenger. Always make your own checks to be sure it's safe to pull out.

Question 22 *

You are driving on a single track road which is only wide enough for one vehicle. What should you do if another car comes towards you?

A   Pull into a passing place on your right

B   Reverse until the road becomes wider

C   Drive onto the grass verge

D   Pull into a passing place on your left

Question 23 *

What does this traffic sign mean?

A   No parking allowed

B   Parking for cars only

C   Only motor cars allowed

D   No motor cars allowed

Answers

Question 22

D - Narrow roads such as this usually have passing places where the road is widened to make room for two vehicles to pass. You should plan well ahead and be prepared to pull into a space on your left. If there is a closer space on your right, you should stop and wait opposite it. Driving onto the grass verge should be avoided wherever possible, as there may be hidden dips or soft earth where you may become stuck.

Question 23

D - Drivers of motor cars are not allowed to proceed beyond this sign.

Question 24

What should you do if you're signalled to stop by a police officer in a patrol car?

A   Stop on the left as soon as it's safe

B   Wait until they turn on the blue light before stopping

C   Carry on until you reach a side road

D   Stop immediately wherever you are

Question 25 *

What should you do before making a journey when it is snowing?

A   Ask yourself whether you really need to travel

B   Avoid carrying too many passengers

C   Plan a route avoiding open roads

D   Make sure that your air conditioning is working

Question 26 *

Just ahead of you there is bus which has pulled into a stop. You are not sure when it will move off. What should you do?

A   Stop and wait to see what happens

B   Drive past the bus with caution

C   Accelerate to get quickly past

D   Sound the horn or flash your lights

Answers

Question 24

A - If a police officer signals for you to stop, keep calm, think before you act, and stop as soon as possible in a safe place on the left.

Question 25

A - Driving in snow should always be avoided wherever possible. There is always a greater risk of accidents and breakdowns when the weather is bad. You need to ask yourself if you really do need to travel.

Question 26

B - You should carry on past the bus but proceed with caution in case the driver signals or begins to move off. There may also be passengers about to step out so keep your speed in hand and your eyes open.

Question 27

On a motorway, what is an emergency refuge area used for?

A   When your vehicle has a serious problem

B   If you think you'll be involved in a road rage incident

C   For a police patrol to park and watch traffic

D   For construction and road workers to store emergency equipment

Question 28 *

You are driving on the left of this road. When may you cross the centre lines?

A   You must not cross them at all

B   When overtaking another driver

C   When passing an obstruction

D   When you can see it is clear ahead

Answers

Question 27

A - Emergency refuge areas are built at the side of the hard shoulder. If you break down, try to get your vehicle into the refuge, where there's an emergency telephone. The phone connects directly to a control centre. Remember to take care when rejoining the motorway, especially if the hard shoulder is being used as a running lane.

Question 28

C - With double white lines, if the nearest line to you is solid then you may only cross it in certain circumstances. One of those is if you have to pass a stationary obstruction.

Question 29 *

You see a learner driver starting to pull out of a junction close on your left. What action should you take?

A   Reduce speed and be ready to pull back in case they continue

B   Carry on as normal as their instructor will stop them

C   Slow down and wave them out of the junction

D   Move into a wide position so that you can pass them if they pull out

Question 30 *

You are on a busy dual-carriageway; the following driver is much too close to your rear. What can you do to lower the risk?

A   Increase the gap between you and the vehicle ahead

B   Pick up speed to increase the distance behind

C   Slow right down until the other driver overtakes

D   Signal left to let the other driver know they can overtake

Question 31

What's the purpose of a catalytic converter?

A   To reduce the risk of fire

B   To reduce fuel consumption

C   To reduce harmful exhaust gases

D   To reduce engine wear

Answers

Question 29

A - Learner drivers can be unpredictable and may lose control of the car. You should be courteous and maintain a safe distance, allowing for any mistakes that they might make. Never wave other road users on; you may put them into danger from someone else.

Question 30

A - If they wish to overtake at any point, you should leave that decision up to them and maintain a steady speed while gradually opening up space ahead. If you have plenty of space in front, then you will have more time to react if traffic suddenly slows down. This will lessen the risk of the following driver running into you.

Question 31

C - Catalytic converters reduce a large percentage of harmful exhaust emissions. They work more efficiently when the engine has reached its normal working temperature.

Question 32

You are convicted of driving after drinking too much alcohol. How could this affect your insurance?

A   Your insurance may become invalid

B   The amount of excess you pay will be reduced

C   You will only be able to get third-party cover

D   Cover will only be given for driving smaller cars

Question 33 *

This blue sign on a yellow background has flashing amber lights. Where would it be displayed?

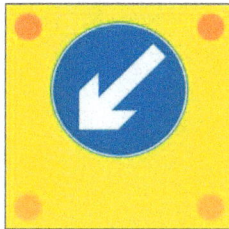

A   In a one-way street

B   On the back of a slow moving vehicle

C   On a traffic island

D   At the entrance to a tunnel

Answers

Question 32

A - Driving while under the influence of drink or drugs can invalidate your insurance. It also endangers yourself and others. The risk isn't worth taking.

Question 33

B - It will be seen on the back of a slow moving vehicle which will probably be involved in carriageway repairs or improvements. The arrow indicates that you should pass the vehicle on its left hand side.

Question 34

What should you do as you approach this overhead bridge?

A   Move out to the centre of the road before going through

B   Find another route; this one is only for high vehicles

C   Be prepared for large vehicles in the middle of the road

D   Move across to the right-hand side before going through

Question 35

When it is particularly important to check the engine oil level?

A   Before a long journey

B   When the engine is hot

C   Early in the morning

D   Every 6000 miles

Answers

Question 34

C - Oncoming large vehicles may need to move to the middle of the road to pass safely under the bridge. There won't be enough room for you to continue, so you should be ready to stop and wait.

Question 35

A - An engine can use more oil during long journeys than on shorter trips. Insufficient engine oil is potentially dangerous: it can lead to excessive wear, mechanical breakdown and expensive repairs. Many modern vehicles have electronic systems to display the oil level. Refer to your manufacturer handbook for instructions if you're not sure how to check your oil.

Question 36 *

Vehicles over a certain age must have yearly MOT test. Why is this?

A   To ensure that it is mechanically safe

B   To monitor its fuel consumption

C   To check that the owner has the necessary documents

D   To check that it has been serviced

Question 37 *

What type of vehicle might you see with a flashing green light on top?

A   An agricultural vehicle

B   A road sweeper

C   An invalid carriage

D   An emergency doctor's car

Question 38

You've broken down on a motorway. In which direction should you walk to find the nearest emergency telephone?

A   With the traffic flow

B   In the direction shown on the marker posts

C   Facing oncoming traffic

D   In the direction of the nearest exit

Answers

Question 36

A - Most vehicles have to take an MOT test every year once they are over three years old. This is to ensure that they are mechanically sound and safe to use on the roads.

Question 37

D - A doctor is allowed to put a flashing green light on top of their car when they are on an emergency call. If you see one of these you should give way to them if you can do so safely.

Question 38

B - Along the hard shoulder there are marker posts at 100-metre intervals. These will direct you to the nearest emergency telephone

Question 39

What restrictions apply to new drivers holding a provisional driving licence?

A   They can't drive over 30 mph

B   They can't drive at night

C   They can't drive unaccompanied

D   They can't drive with more than one passenger

Question 40 *

Why do some motorways have variable speed limits?

A   To reduce traffic bunching at peak times

B   To encourage eco-safe driving methods

C   To compensate for poor road surfaces

D   To keep noise down when passing urban areas

Answers

Question 39

C - You won't be able to drive unaccompanied until you've passed your practical driving test. When you've passed, it's a good idea to ask your instructor to take you for a lesson on the motorway. Alternatively, you could take part in the Pass Plus scheme. This has been created for new drivers and includes motorway driving. Ask your instructor for details.

Question 40

A - Variable speed limits are used when traffic is busy, and when there are incidents and lane closures. This helps to keep traffic moving at a steady varying speed instead of the 'stop start' situation which normally occurs at these times.

Question 41

The road outside this school is marked with yellow zig-zag lines. What do these lines mean?

A   You may wait here when dropping off schoolchildren

B   You may park here when picking up schoolchildren

C   You mustn't wait or park your vehicle here at all

D   You must stay with your vehicle if you park here

Question 42

What does this sign mean?

A   Side winds

B   Airport ahead

C   Slippery road

D   Flooding

Answers

Question 41

C - Parking here would block other road users' view of the school entrance and would endanger the lives of children on their way to and from school.

Question 42

A - You may see this sign in areas where the road is surrounded by open ground. You need to be aware that strong crosswinds could blow you off course.

Question 43 *

What does this road sign mean?

A   No parking on the right

B   No cars are allowed

C   Two-way traffic

D   No overtaking

Question 44

Which of the following types of glasses shouldn't be worn when driving at night?

A   Half-moon

B   Varifocal

C   Bifocal

D   Tinted

Answers

Question 43

D - You must not overtake any other motor vehicle when you see this sign by the road.

Question 44

D - If you're driving at night or in poor visibility, tinted lenses will reduce the efficiency of your vision by reducing the amount of light reaching your eyes.

Question 45

You're parking your car facing uphill with a kerb on your left. You apply the parking brake. What else should you do for added security?

A   Leave the front wheels turned to the left, with the vehicle in first gear

B   Leave the front wheels turned to the left, with the vehicle in reverse gear

C   Leave the front wheels turned to the right, with the vehicle in first gear

D   Leave the front wheels turned to the right, with the vehicle in reverse gear

Question 46 *

Which of the following will have an effect on the stopping distance of your car?

A   The traffic ahead of you

B   The condition of your tyres

C   The light conditions

D   The position of following traffic

Answers

Question 45

C - Should the parking brake fail, the use of first gear will help to prevent the vehicle from rolling backwards. By turning the front wheels to the right, they'll travel the shortest distance before running against the kerb. This will reduce the potential for the vehicle to move any further.

Question 46

B - There are a number of factors which will affect the distance it takes for you to stop. One of the most important is the condition of your tyres. You should make a regular check to ensure that they are in good condition and have a good amount of tread on them.

Question 47 *

What does this sign mean?

A   No motor vehicles

B   Motor cars and motorcycles only

C   Motorcycles have priority

D   All vehicles prohibited

Question 48 *

What does this warning light on the instrument panel mean?

A   Low oil pressure

B   Battery discharge

C   Braking-system fault

D   A door is open

Answers

Question 47

A - The sign prohibits all motor vehicles from proceeding. Cyclists, horse drawn carriages etc. are still allowed to continue.

Question 48

C - If this warning sign lights up on your dashboard you should call for help and get your brake system checked immediately.

Question 49

You're driving on a motorway. The car in front shows its hazard warning lights for a short time. What does this tell you?

A   There's a police speed check ahead

B   The driver wants you to overtake

C   The other car is going to change lanes

D   Traffic ahead is slowing or stopping suddenly

Question 50

You intend to turn right into a side road. Why should you check for motorcyclists just before turning?

A   They may be overtaking on your right

B   They may be emerging from the side road

C   They may be following you closely

D   They may be overtaking on your left

Answers

Question 49

D - If the vehicle in front shows its hazard warning lights, there may be an incident, stopped traffic or queuing traffic ahead. By keeping a safe distance from the vehicle in front, you're able to look beyond it and see any hazards well ahead.

Question 50

A - Never attempt to change direction to the right without first checking your right-hand mirror and blind spot. A motorcyclist might not have seen your signal and could be hidden by other traffic. This observation should become a matter of routine.

The Learner Driver's Logbook

Lesson & Progress Record

UK Driving Skills

Test Four

Question 1

You're travelling in very heavy rain. How is this likely to affect your overall stopping distance?

A   It will be halved

B   It will be five times longer

C   It will be about the same

D   It will be doubled

Question 2 *

You want to continue ahead at a crossroads where there are no road markings. There are other vehicles approaching from your right and left. Who has priority?

A   No-one has priority

B   The faster vehicle

C   The vehicle on the left

D   The vehicle on the right

Question 3

You're parked in a busy high street. What's the safest way to turn your vehicle around so you can go the opposite way?

A   Drive into a side road and reverse into the main road

B   Get someone to stop the traffic

C   Do a u-turn

D   Find a side road to turn around in

Answers

Question 1

D - The road will be very wet and spray from other vehicles will reduce your visibility. Tyre grip will also be reduced, increasing your stopping distance. You should at least double your separation distance.

Question 2

A - No-one has priority in this situation. Unmarked crossroads should be approached with plenty of caution. Slow down, take good observation in all directions before you emerge or make a turn. Proceed only when you're sure it's safe to do so.

Question 3

D - Make sure you carry out the manoeuvre without causing a hazard to other vehicles. Choose a place to turn that's safe and convenient for you and for other road users.

Question 4 *

Which of these is likely to be the cause of excessive or uneven tyre wear?

A   Crossing your hands when steering

B   Incorrect use of the gears

C   A fault in the braking system

D   Incorrect operation of the clutch

Question 5 *

What should you do to avoid wheel-spin when driving on ice and snow?

A   By avoiding use of the parking brake

B   By using higher gears than normal

C   By using the ABS braking system

D   By staying in low gears

Question 6 *

When is it acceptable to turn on front fog lights?

A   As soon as mist begins to form

B   As a replacement for main beam headlights

C   When it is starting to get dark

D   When visibility is seriously reduced

Answers

Question 4

C - If you see that parts of the tread on your tyres are wearing before others, it may indicate a brake, steering or suspension fault. Regular servicing will help to detect faults at an early stage and this will avoid the risk of minor faults becoming serious or even dangerous.

Question 5

B - There is less turn of the wheels for any given amount of acceleration when using a higher gear. If you're travelling on an icy road, extra caution will be required to avoid loss of control. Keeping your speed down and using the highest gear possible will reduce the risk of the tyres losing their grip on this slippery surface.

Question 6

D - It is against the law to use fog lights except when visibility is 'seriously reduced'; that is down to less than 100 m (328 feet). If they are used in better conditions they can dazzle other road users. You should make sure when you do have to use them, that you turn them off again as soon as visibility improves.

Question 7

How long after first registration must a car have its first MOT test?

A   One year

B   Five years

C   Three years

D   Seven years

Question 8 *

You are waiting behind a cyclist at traffic lights. What should you do when the lights change to green?

A   Move off quickly to pass the cyclist

B   Sound your horn before passing them

C   Stay close behind them as you move off

D   Hold back to give them time to move off

Question 9

How will a heavy load attached to the roof rack affect the handling of your car?

A   It will reduce the stopping distance

B   It will reduce stability

C   It will make the steering lighter

D   It will improve the road holding

Answers

Question 7

C - Any car you drive must be in good condition and roadworthy. If it's over three years old, it must have a valid MOT test certificate (unless it's exempt from the MOT test - see GOV.UK).

Question 8

D - Cyclists can be unstable when they first set off and may wobble. You should give them time to get moving, and then give them plenty of space when you pass.

Question 9

B - A heavy load on your roof rack will reduce the stability of the vehicle because it moves the centre of gravity away from that designed by the manufacturer. Be aware of this when you drive round bends and corners. If you change direction at speed, your vehicle and/or load could become unstable and you could lose control.

Question 10

What does this sign mean?

A   End of cycle route

B   End of clearway

C   End of restricted speed area

D   End of restricted parking area

Question 11

You're carrying a child in your car. They're under three years old. Which of these is a suitable restraint?

A   A child seat

B   An adult lap belt

C   An adult holding a child

D   A normal seat belt

Answers

Question 10

D - Even though you've left the restricted area, make sure that you park where you won't endanger other road users or cause an obstruction.

Question 11

A - Suitable restraints include a child seat, baby seat, booster seat or booster cushion. It's essential that any restraint used is suitable for the child's size and weight, and fitted according to the manufacturer's instructions.

Question 12 *

You are going to be driving a long distance at motorway speeds. Your car is carrying passengers and luggage. What should you do to the tyre pressures?

A   Reduce pressure in all the tyres

B   Increase pressure in the rear tyres

C   Increase pressure in all the tyres

D   Reduce pressure in the rear tyres

Question 13 *

Your car has a reversing camera. How should you make use of this?

A   You can use it in place of looking round to the rear of the car

B   You should only use it when the car is stationary

C   You should only use it when there is something behind you

D   You can use it in addition to taking observation around the car

Question 14

What does a sign with a brown background show?

A   Primary roads

B   Minor roads

C   Tourist directions

D   Urban motorway route

Answers

Question 12

C - When driving at higher speeds, there is more stress on the tyres, therefore inflating them to a higher pressure will give them more support over a long journey. This is particularly important when you are also carrying a heavy load. Check your vehicle handbook for guidance.

Question 13

D - Reversing cameras are useful aids but they don't always give a full field of vision and the view is often distorted. They can be used to aid observation when reversing, but at no time should you neglect to take proper observation all around the car.

Question 14

C - Signs with a brown background give directions to places of interest. They're often seen on a motorway, directing you along the easiest route to the attraction.

Question 15 *

At a crossroads, you see a square box with criss-cross yellow lines painted on the road. What do these markings mean?

A   This is where you must stop when the lights change

B   It is there to guide you into the correct position

C   It is reserved for emergency vehicles

D   The painted area must not be blocked

Question 16 *

You want to turn right from a one-way street. Where should you position your car?

A   Well to the right of the road

B   Well to the left of the road

C   Just left of the road centre

D   It doesn't matter in a one-way street

Question 17 *

You have a hand held mobile phone in your vehicle. What should you do to make a call whilst in traffic?

A   Dial the number and then put the handset back into a cradle

B   Find a safe place to stop before you pick the phone up

C   Wait until you're stationary at traffic lights

D   Pull up on double yellow lines with your hazard lights on

Answers

Question 15

D - Yellow box junctions are designed to keep junctions clear. You should not enter it if your exit from it is blocked (except when turning right, providing it is only oncoming traffic which is preventing you from completing the turn).

Question 16

A - In a one-way street you should position on the right hand side, and take up this position as soon as you can to make sure that no-one can come up on the outside of you.

Question 17

B - It is unsafe and against the law to use a hand held phone while driving, even when stationary in traffic queues. You MUST find a safe place to pull over and stop before using it and that does not include double yellow lines which indicate that waiting restrictions apply.

Question 18 *

It is a bright and sunny day. You are about to drive through a tunnel. What should you do before you enter it?

A   Turn off the radio

B   Take of your sunglasses

C   Switch off your mobile phone

D   Turn on the demisters

Question 19

Your vehicle is insured third-party only. What does this cover?

A   All damage and injury

B   Damage to other vehicles

C   Damage to your vehicle

D   Injury to yourself

Question 20

What does 'tailgating' mean?

A   Driving with rear fog lights on

B   Following another vehicle too closely

C   Reversing into a parking space

D   Using the rear door of a hatchback car

Answers

Question 18

B - Tunnels can be quite dark; you need to be able to see properly so if you are wearing sunglasses they should be removed until you reach the end.

Question 19

B - Third-party insurance cover is usually cheaper than comprehensive cover. However, it doesn't cover any damage caused to your own vehicle or property. It only covers damage and injury you cause to others.

Question 20

B - 'Tailgating' is the term used when a driver or rider follows the vehicle in front too closely. It's dangerous because it restricts their view of the road ahead and leaves no safety margin if the vehicle in front needs to slow down or stop suddenly. Tailgating is often the underlying cause of rear-end collisions or multiple pile-ups.

Question 21

What should the driver of the grey car on the left (arrowed) be especially aware of?

A   Doors opening on parked cars

B   The right-hand kerb

C   The uneven road surface

D   Overhanging trees

Question 22

There are no speed-limit signs on the road. How is a 30 mph limit indicated?

A   By double or single yellow lines

B   By hazard warning lines

C   By pedestrian islands

D   By street lighting

Answers

Question 21

A - When passing parked cars, there's a risk that a driver or passenger may not check before opening the door into the road. A defensive driver will drive slowly and be looking for people who may be about to get out of their car.

Question 22

D - There's a 30 mph speed limit where there are street lights unless signs show another limit.

Question 23 *

What do these road markings mean?

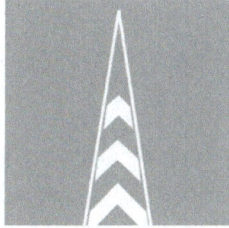

A   Keep two chevrons apart

B   One way street

C   Do not cross

D   Speed humps

Question 24

What does this sign mean?

A   11 tonne weight limit

B   Right-hand lane T-junction

C   Right-hand lane closed ahead

D   Through traffic to use left lane

Answers

Question 23

C - These markings are seen on a motorway separating lanes, normally where a slip road joins the motorway or where motorways separate. You MUST not cross these where the border is solid except in an unavoidable emergency.

Question 24

C - You should change lanes as directed by the sign. Here, the right-hand lane is closed but the left-hand and centre lanes are available. Merging in turn is recommended when it's safe and traffic is going slowly; for example, at roadworks or a road traffic incident. When vehicles are travelling at speed, this isn't advisable and you should move into the appropriate lane in good time.

Question 25

Where should you not use a breakdown warning triangle?

A   On a dual carriageway

B   On a single-track road

C   On a narrow country road

D   On a motorway

Question 26

You are on a three-lane motorway. There are red reflective studs on your left and white ones to your right. Which lane are you in?

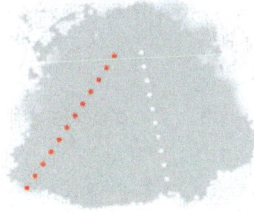

A   In the left-hand lane

B   In the middle lane

C   In the right-hand lane

D   On the hard shoulder

Answers

Question 25

D - If your vehicle breaks down, be aware of the danger to, and from, other traffic. Get your vehicle off the road if possible. Use a warning triangle to alert other road users to the obstruction but NOT when you're on a motorway. The risk of walking along the hard shoulder to place the triangle is too great.

Question 26

A - The colours of the reflective studs on the motorway and their locations are:

- red – between the hard shoulder and the carriageway
- white – between lanes
- amber – between the carriageway and the central reservation
- green – along slip-road exits and entrances
- bright green/yellow – at roadworks and contraflow systems.

Question 27

The fluid level in your battery is low. What should you top it up with?

A   Battery acid

B   Distilled water

C   Engine coolant

D   Engine oil

Question 28

What must you have when you apply to renew your vehicle tax?

A   A valid driving licence

B   The handbook

C   The vehicle's chassis number

D   Valid insurance

Question 29

Overall stopping distance is made up of thinking distance and braking distance. You are on a good, dry road surface, with good brakes and tyres. What is the typical braking distance from 50 mph?

A   14 metres (46 feet)

B   24 metres (80 feet)

C   38 metres (125 feet)

D   55 metres (180 feet)

Answers

Question 27

B - Many modern batteries are now maintenance-free. Check your vehicle handbook and, if necessary, make sure that the plates in each battery cell are covered with fluid.

Question 28

D - You can renew your vehicle tax online, at post offices and vehicle registration offices, or by phone. When applying, make sure you have all the relevant valid documents, including a valid MOT test certificate where applicable.

Question 29

C - Be aware that this is just the braking distance. You need to add the thinking distance to this to give the overall stopping distance. At 50 mph, the typical thinking distance will be 15 metres (50 feet), plus a braking distance of 38 metres (125 feet), giving an overall stopping distance of 53 metres (175 feet). The stopping distance could be greater than this, depending on your attention and response to any hazards. These figures are a general guide.

Question 30

You are involved in a collision. Afterwards, which document may the police ask you to produce?

A   Driving licence

B   Theory test certificate

C   Vehicle registration document

D   Vehicle service record

Question 31

What must you make sure of before you drive someone else's vehicle?

A   That the insurance documents are in the vehicle

B   That the vehicle is insured for your use

C   That the vehicle owner has third-party insurance cover

D   That your own vehicle has insurance cover

Question 32

Your vehicle catches fire while driving through a tunnel. It is still driveable. What should you do?

A   Drive it out of the tunnel if you can do so

B   Leave it where it is, with the engine running

C   Stop, and wait for help to arrive

D   Pull up, then walk to an emergency telephone

Answers

Question 30

A - You must stop if you've been involved in a collision which results in injury or damage. The police may ask to see your driving licence and insurance details at the time or later at a police station.

Question 31

B - Driving a vehicle without insurance cover is illegal, so be sure that, whoever's car you drive, you're insured – whether on their policy or on your own. If you need to take out insurance, it's worth comparing several quotes before you decide which insurance provider best meets your needs.

Question 32

A - If it's possible, and you can do so without causing further danger, it may be safer to drive a vehicle that's on fire out of a tunnel. The greatest danger in a tunnel fire is smoke and suffocation.

Question 33

After passing your driving test, you suffer from ill health which affects your driving. What must you do?

A   Always drive accompanied

B   Avoid using motorways

C   Inform the licensing authority

D   Inform your local police

Question 34

When is it acceptable for a passenger to travel in a car without wearing a seat belt?

A   When they are exempt for medical reasons

B   When they are sitting in the rear seat

C   When they are under 1.5 metres (5 feet) in height

D   When they are under 14 years old

Answers

Question 33

C - You must tell DVLA (or DVA in Northern Ireland) if your health is likely to affect your ability to drive. The licensing authority will investigate your situation and then make a decision on whether or not to take away your licence.

Question 34

A - Where fitted, seat belts must be worn. It's the driver's responsibility to ensure that children under 14 years old wear a seat belt or use a suitable child restraint. Passengers aged 14 or over are responsible for wearing their seat belt. Exceptions to this law are made for people who hold a medical exemption certificate.

Question 35

What do these motorway signs show?

A   They warn of a police control ahead

B   They are countdown markers to a bridge

C   They are countdown markers to the next exit

D   They are distance markers to the next telephone

Question 36

Which vehicle is most likely to take an unusual course at a roundabout?

A   Delivery van

B   A taxi

C   Long vehicle

D   An electric vehicle

Answers

Question 35

C - The exit from a motorway is indicated by countdown markers. These are positioned 90 metres (100 yards) apart, the first being 270 metres (300 yards) from the start of the slip road. Move into the left-hand lane well before you reach the start of the slip road.

Question 36

C - Long vehicles might have to take a slightly different position when approaching the roundabout or going around it. This is to stop the rear of the vehicle cutting in and mounting the kerb.

Horse riders and cyclists might stay in the left-hand lane although they're turning right. Be aware of this and allow them room.

Question 37

What does this sign mean?

A   No entry for traffic turning left

B   No through road on the left

C   Turn left for ferry terminal

D   Turn left for parking area

Question 38 *

What would these road markings be used to highlight?

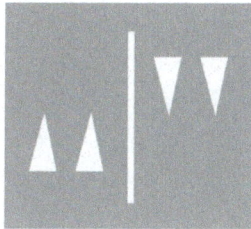

A   A pedestrianised area

B   A pelican crossing

C   A level crossing

D   A hump in the road surface

Answers

Question 37

B - This sign shows you that you can't get through to another route by turning left at the junction ahead.

Question 38

D - Changes in the level of the road surface aren't always easily seen. White triangles such as these painted on the surface give you an indication of where there are road humps.

Question 39

Which of these is a hazard warning line?

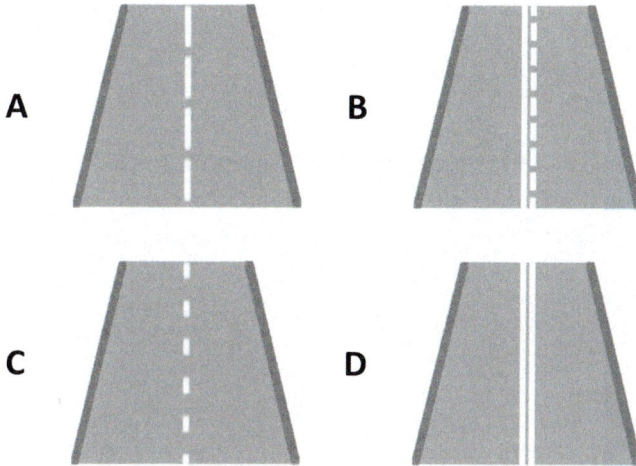

A

B

C

D

Question 40

You're towing a small trailer on a busy three-lane motorway. All lanes are open. Which of these is correct?

A   You must have a stabiliser fitted

B   You must not exceed 50 mph

C   You must not overtake

D   You may only use the left-hand and centre lanes

Answers

Question 39

A - You need to know the difference between the normal centre line and a hazard warning line. If there's a hazard ahead, the markings are longer and the gaps shorter. This gives you advance warning of an unspecified hazard.

Question 40

D - The motorway regulations for towing a trailer state that you must not :

- use the right-hand lane of a three-lane motorway unless directed to do so (for example, at roadworks or due to a lane closure)
- exceed 60 mph.

Question 41 *

You're approaching a set of traffic lights. They have been on green for quite a while. What should you do?

A   Pick up speed before they change

B   Check your mirrors and prepare to stop

C   Change into a lower gear

D   Maintain a steady speed

Question 42

What must you do when overtaking a car at night?

A   Flash your headlights before overtaking

B   Make sure you don't dazzle other road users

C   Avoid using your indicators

D   Switch your lights to full beam before overtaking

Question 43 *

Before you drive on a motorway as a learner, what must you make sure of?

A   That you are in a dual-controlled car with an instructor

B   That your car is capable of exceeding 70 mph

C   That your insurance covers you for motorways

D   That you take the 'L' plates from your car

Answers

Question 41

B - Lights which have green for a long time are possibly about to change. You should check your mirrors, ease off the gas and be ready to stop in case they do.

Question 42

B - To prevent your lights from dazzling the driver of the car in front, wait until you've passed them before switching to full beam.

Question 43

A - Before June 2018 learner drivers were not allowed on motorways. From that date they can practise on motorways providing that they are with an approved driving instructor in a car with dual brakes.

Question 44

You've broken down on a two-way road. You have a warning triangle. At least how far from your vehicle should you place the warning triangle?

A   100 metres (328 feet)

B   25 metres (82 feet)

C   45 metres (147 feet)

D   5 metres (16 feet)

Question 45

Why should you switch off your rear fog lights when the fog has cleared?

A   To allow your headlights to work better

B   To prevent dazzling following drivers

C   To help prevent battery drain

D   To stop the engine losing power

Answers

Question 44

C - Advance warning triangles fold flat and don't take up much room. Use one to warn other road users if your vehicle has broken down or if there has been an incident. Place it at least 45 metres (147 feet) behind your vehicle (or the incident), on the same side of the road or verge. Place it further back if the scene is hidden by, for example, a bend, hill or dip in the road. Don't use warning triangles on motorways.

Question 45

B - Don't forget to switch off your fog lights when the weather improves. You could be prosecuted for driving with them on in good visibility. The high intensity of rear fog lights can dazzle following drivers and make your brake lights difficult to notice.

Question 46

Who's responsible for making sure that a vehicle isn't overloaded?

A   The driver of the vehicle

B   The licensing authority

C   The owner of the items being carried

D   The person who loaded the vehicle

Question 47

You're driving down a long, steep hill. You suddenly notice that your brakes aren't working as well as normal. What's the usual cause of this?

A   Air in the brake fluid

B   Badly adjusted brakes

C   Oil on the brakes

D   The brakes overheating

Answers

Question 46

A - Carrying heavy loads will affect control and the vehicle's handling characteristics. If the vehicle you're driving is overloaded, you'll be held responsible.

Question 47

D - Continuous use of the brakes can cause them to start overheating. This is more likely to happen on vehicles fitted with drum brakes, but it can apply to disc brakes as well. Using a lower gear will assist the braking and help you to keep control of your vehicle.

Question 48

Why are these yellow lines painted across the road?

A   To help you choose the correct lane

B   To help you keep the correct separation distance

C   To make you aware of your speed

D   To tell you the distance to the roundabout

Question 49

What are triangular signs for?

A   To give directions

B   To give speed limits

C   To give orders

D   To give warnings

Answers

Question 48

C - These lines are often found on the approach to a roundabout or a dangerous junction. They give you extra warning to adjust your speed. Look well ahead and do this in good time.

Question 49

D - This type of sign warns you of hazards ahead. Make sure you look at each sign that you pass on the road, so that you don't miss any vital instructions or information.

Question 50 *

You see this sign on a motorway, what is it telling you?

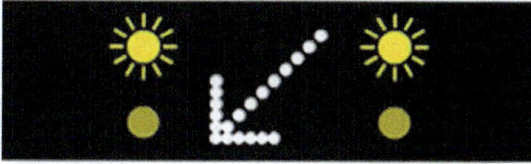

A   You should move to the lane on your left

B   You must not move into the left hand lane

C   You must leave the motorway at the next exit

D   You should move across to the hard shoulder

Answers

Question 50

A - Overhead signs on motorways will give instructions such as temporary speed limits and lane closures. This sign tells you to move into the next lane on your left

The Driving Test
& How to Pass

An Examiner's Guide to the 'L' Test

UK Driving Skills

Test Five

Question 1

When should anti-freeze be used in the cooling system?

A   In winter only

B   In autumn and winter

C   Only when it is icy

D   All year round

Question 2

You're on a motorway. Red flashing lights appear above your lane only. What should you do?

A   Move into another lane in good time

B   Continue in that lane and look for further information

C   Pull onto the hard shoulder

D   Stop and wait for an instruction to proceed

Question 3

What should you do if you're feeling tired but there's nowhere to stop safely?

A   Ensure a supply of fresh air

B   Increase your speed to find a stopping place more quickly

C   Stop anyway as you need to rest

D   Keep changing speed to improve your concentration

Answers

Question 1

D - Today, all water-cooled engines use a mixture of water and anti-freeze to make up the coolant. As well as helping to keep the engine at its correct operating temperature, the anti-freeze acts as a corrosion inhibitor to prolong the life of the cooling system.

Question 2

A - Flashing red lights above your lane show that your lane is closed. You should move into another lane as soon as it's safe to do so.

Question 3

A - If you're travelling on a long journey, plan your route before you leave. This will help you to

- be decisive at junctions
- plan your rest stops
- know approximately how long your journey will take.

Make sure that the vehicle you're travelling in is well ventilated. A warm, stuffy atmosphere can make you drowsy, which will impair your judgement and perception.

Question 4

You're driving downhill. How will this affect your vehicle?

A   It will need more engine power

B   It will take longer to stop

C   It will increase fuel consumption

D   It will be easier to change direction

Question 5 *

After using the right-hand lane of a motorway to overtake, when would it be wise to stay in that lane instead of moving promptly back to the left?

A   When you want to continue driving at a higher speed

B   When there is nothing following close behind you

C   When the driver you have passed flashes their lights

D   When vehicles are bunching up together in the left-hand lane

Answers

Question 4

B - When driving downhill, gravity will cause the vehicle to increase speed. More braking effort will be required, and stopping distances will increase

Question 5

D - After overtaking you should normally always move back to the lane on your left as soon as it's safe to do so. If you see vehicles bunching up in the left-hand lane however; this could be a sign that one or more of them may be about to pull out to overtake. In this situation you should stay in the right-hand lane until you're sure it's safe to move back to your left.

Question 6

What does this motorway sign mean?

A   You're approaching a long downhill slope

B   You're approaching a long uphill slope

C   You're approaching a 'lorries only' lane

D   You're approaching a service area

Question 7 *

You're planning to overtake on a single carriageway road. What do you need to be aware of?

A   That there may be junctions ahead

B   That you need to keep close to the other vehicle before pulling out

C   That the other driver may wave you past

D   That you mustn't exceed the speed limit by more than 10mph

Answers

Question 6

B - The term 'crawler lane' doesn't mean the lane is only for extremely slow vehicles. It's advising you of an extra lane on the left. Crawler lanes are usually built on sections of road where the length of the gradient is such that some large vehicles will be slowed to the point where they become a hazard for other road users.

Question 7

A - Before overtaking, you need to make sure it's safe to carry out the manoeuvre. As part of your check, look well ahead for road junctions. You shouldn't overtake as you approach a road junction, because if a vehicle emerges, or has to wait to turn, you could risk a collision.

Question 8

You're in the left-hand lane on a three-lane motorway. Why should you check for any vehicles in the right-hand lane before you overtake?

A   They may be moving faster than you

B   They may cut in sharply behind you

C   They may accelerate briskly in front of you

D   They may move back to the middle lane as you move out

Question 9

You're at a road junction, turning into a minor road. What should you do if there are pedestrians crossing the minor road?

A   Stop and wave the pedestrians across

B   Sound your horn to let the pedestrians know that you're there

C   Give way to the pedestrians who are already crossing

D   Carry on; the pedestrians should give way to you

Question 10 *

Why is it a good idea to switch to a local radio station before entering a tunnel?

A   Because the local radio content will be better

B   Because national radio signals will be lost

C   Because it will be compatible with your sat nav

D   Because it may give you information about any problems ahead

Answers

Question 8

D - Vehicles overtaking in the right-hand lane may return to the centre lane when they've finished their manoeuvre. You should look for this before starting to pull out.

Question 9

C - Always look into the road you're entering. If pedestrians are already crossing, be considerate and give way to them. Don't wave or signal them to hurry; they have priority here.

Question 10

D - On the approach to many tunnels, a board will indicate a local channel or radio frequency that you should tune into. This should give a warning of any incident or congestion in the tunnel ahead. Severe loss of life has occurred in tunnel fires. Getting advance warning of any problems ahead will help you to take appropriate action in good time.

Question 11

What should you do if a front tyre bursts while you're driving on a motorway?

A   Loosen your grip on the steering wheel

B   Brake firmly to a stop

C   Hold the steering wheel firmly

D   Drive to the next service area

Question 12

A bus has stopped at a bus stop ahead of you. What should you do if its right-hand indicator is flashing?

A   Flash your headlights and slow down

B   Sound your horn and keep going

C   Slow down and then sound your horn

D   Slow down and give way if it's safe to do so

Question 13 *

You're waiting to turn right into a side road. An oncoming driver slows down and flashes their lights. What should you do?

A   Make the turn as quickly as possible

B   Ignore the other driver and stay where you are

C   Make the turn after checking that it's safe to do so

D   Stay where you are and wave the other driver on

Answers

Question 11

C - A front tyre bursting will seriously reduce your control of the vehicle. Keep calm and resist the temptation to brake hard or swerve. Hold the steering wheel firmly and try to get the vehicle onto the hard shoulder while allowing it to slow down gradually. Stop as far to the left as possible and switch on your hazard warning lights.

Question 12

D - Give way to buses whenever you can do so safely, especially when they signal to pull away from bus stops. Look out for people who have left the bus and wish to cross the road. Also look for people rushing to catch a bus: they may be more concerned about catching the bus than watching for traffic.

Question 13

C - The flashing of headlights has the same meaning as sounding the horn: it's a warning of someone's presence. However many drivers misuse it as a signal for another driver to go ahead. Before turning you need to be aware of certain things:

- That the signal is meant for you

- That the other driver is definitely waiting

- That there are no pedestrians crossing the side road

- That no other vehicles are about to pass the other driver, particularly cyclists and motorcyclists who may be hidden from view.

Question 14

You're testing your suspension. You notice that your vehicle keeps bouncing when you press down on the front wing. What does this mean?

A   Worn tyres

B   Tyres under-inflated

C   Steering wheel not located centrally

D   Worn shock absorbers

Question 15

Which of the following may help to deter a thief from stealing your car?

A   Parking near to other vehicles for security

B   Fitting tinted windows to make it difficult to see inside

C   Using a 'No valuables left inside' sticker on the window

D   Etching the registration number on the windows

Question 16

You have too much oil in your engine. What could this cause?

A   Oil leaks

B   Low oil pressure

C   Engine overheating

D   Carburettor damage

Answers

Question 14

D - If you find that your vehicle bounces as you drive around a corner or bend in the road, the shock absorbers might be worn. Press down on the front wing and, if the vehicle continues to bounce, take it to be checked by a qualified mechanic.

Question 15

D - Having your car registration number etched on all your windows is a cheap and effective way to deter professional car thieves. This would mean that they would have to go to the expense of replacing all the glass if they tried to sell it on.

Question 16

A - Too much oil in the engine will create excess pressure and could damage engine seals and cause oil leaks. Any excess oil should be drained off.

Question 17

How should you overtake a long, slow-moving vehicle on a busy road?

A Follow it closely and keep moving out to see the road ahead

B Edge out so that the oncoming traffic gives way

C Stay behind until the driver waves you past

D Keep well back until you can see that it's clear

Question 18 *

What is the best way to drive your vehicle through a ford?

A Drive through slowly in low gear

B Drive through quickly in low gear

C Drive through slowly in high gear

D Drive through quickly in high gear

Answers

Question 17

D - When you're following a long vehicle, stay well back so that you can get a better view of the road ahead. The closer you get, the less you'll be able to see of the road. Be patient and don't take a gamble. Only overtake when you're certain that you can complete the manoeuvre safely.

Question 18

A - In normal conditions, a ford can be crossed quite safely by driving through it slowly. You need to prevent water from entering through the exhaust by keeping the 'revs' high in a low gear.

Question 19 *

You're travelling at 70 mph in the left-hand lane of a three-lane motorway. What should you do when there are vehicles about to join from the slip road?

A   Speed up to get past them

B   Maintain a steady speed

C   Quickly brake to give way to them

D   Move to another lane if you can

Question 20 *

A cycle lane is marked by a solid white line. What does this mean?

A   Drivers can use it only when parking

B   Drivers must not use that lane at any time

C   Drivers may use the lane at any time

D   Drivers may only use the lane at certain times

Question 21 *

You're driving at night with your headlights on full beam. A vehicle is about to overtake you. When should you dip your lights?

A   Shortly after the vehicle has passed you

B   You should dip them immediately

C   Only if the other driver dips their headlights

D   As soon as the vehicle is about to pass you

Answers

Question 19

D - Plan well ahead when approaching a slip road. If you see traffic joining the motorway, move to another lane if it's safe to do so. This can help the flow of traffic joining the motorway, especially at peak times. You must be careful however not to change lanes unsafely and cause problems for other drivers behind you.

Question 20

B - Cycle lanes which are marked with a continuous solid white line are for cyclists only. You must not drive or ride a motorcycle along it any time. Nor should you park within this area.

Question 21

D - Leaving them on full beam for a few moments as they are pulling out will light the way ahead, but dip your lights as soon as the driver is about to pass you.

Question 22

There's been a collision. A driver is suffering from shock. What should you do?

A   Give them a drink

B   Ask who caused the incident

C   Leave them alone to recover

D   Try to reassure them

Question 23 *

Where should you never consider overtaking a cyclist?

A   On a left-hand bend

B   Just before you turn right

C   Just before you turn left

D   On a right-hand bend

Question 24

What should you do when you're overtaking at night?

A   Wait until a bend so that you can see oncoming headlights

B   Flash your lights before moving out

C   Put your headlights on full beam

D   Beware of bends in the road ahead

Answers

Question 22

D - A casualty suffering from shock may have injuries that aren't immediately obvious. Call the emergency services, then stay with the person in shock, offering reassurance until the experts arrive.

Question 23

C - If there is a cyclist just ahead of you as you approach a junction you should **never** overtake just before turning left. Keep a safe distance behind and allow the rider to pass the junction before you turn.

Even when you're turning right you still need to exercise caution. You may be able to overtake safely if the road is wide enough but always be aware that the rider may also decide to turn right. Hold back if you are in any doubt.

Question 24

D - Don't overtake if there's a possibility of a road junction, bend or brow of a bridge or hill ahead. There are many hazards that are difficult to see in the dark. Only overtake if you're certain that the road ahead is clear. Don't take a chance.

Question 25

Up to how much more fuel will you use by driving at 70 mph, compared with driving at 50 mph?

A   5%

B   15%

C   75%

D   100%

Question 26

What fault would you suspect if the footbrake on your car starts to feel spongy?

A   The wrong brake pads are fitted

B   The brake pads are worn

C   The hydraulic system contains air

D   The brake discs are worn

Question 27

What should you check when you're leaving a motorway after travelling at speed for some time?

A   The speedometer

B   The fuel level

C   The engine temperature

D   The brakes

Answers

Question 25

A - Your vehicle will use less fuel if you avoid heavy acceleration. The higher the engine revs, the more fuel you'll use. Using the same gear, and covering the same distance, a vehicle travelling at 70 mph will use about 15% more fuel than it would at 50 mph. However, don't travel so slowly that you inconvenience or endanger other road users.

Question 26

C - If air gets into the hydraulic system, the brake pedal will feel spongy. When you press it, the air is compressed, causing the pedal to move further than normal. As a result, braking efficiency is reduced. Have the system checked by a qualified mechanic: brake faults are too important to be ignored.

Question 27

A - After leaving a motorway or when using a link road between motorways, your speed may be higher than you realise: 50 mph may feel like 30 mph. Check the speedometer and adjust your speed accordingly. Some slip roads and link roads have sharp bends, so you'll need to slow down.

Question 28

While driving at night, you see a pedestrian ahead. What does it mean if they're wearing reflective clothing and carrying a red light?

A   You're approaching men at work

B   You're approaching an incident black-spot

C   You're approaching slow-moving vehicles

D   You're approaching an organised walk

Question 29

How will a school crossing patrol signal you to stop?

A   By holding up a sign

B   By pointing to children on the opposite pavement

C   By displaying a light

D   By giving you an arm signal

Question 30 *

Where are motorcyclists and cyclists particularly vulnerable?

A   At junctions

B   On dual carriageways

C   On country roads

D   In urban areas

Answers

Question 28

D - Pedestrians who are part of an organised walk using the road at night should wear bright or reflective clothing. The walker in front should display a white light, while the one at the back should display a red light. Be particularly careful, slow down and give the walkers plenty of room.

Question 29

A - If a school crossing patrol holds up a 'stop' sign or steps out into the road with it, you must stop and allow schoolchildren to cross.

Question 30

A - Motorcyclists and cyclists who may be nearer to the kerb than other vehicles can be harder to see when you're emerging from a junction. Their relatively smaller size means that they can also be hidden from view by obstructions such as parked cars and 'street furniture'.

Question 31

What's the maximum fine for driving without insurance?

A   £500

B   Unlimited

C   £1000

D   £5000

Question 32 *

What's the first thing you should do when you see a hazard ahead?

A   Brake firmly

B   Check your mirrors

C   Change into neutral

D   Signal to go around it

Question 33

What does it mean if the signs at a bus lane show no times of operation?

A   The lane isn't in operation

B   The lane is only in operation at peak times

C   The lane is only in operation in daylight hours

D   The lane is in operation 24 hours a day

Answers

Question 31

B - It's a serious offence to drive without insurance. As well as an unlimited fine, you may be disqualified or given penalty points.

Question 32

B - You should always be looking well ahead to spot any hazards which may affect you. Check your mirrors first to assess what following traffic is doing as you may need to make a change of speed or direction.

Question 33

D - Bus -lane signs show the vehicles allowed to use the lane and also its times of operation. Where no times are shown, the bus lane is in operation 24 hours a day.

Question 34

You want to put a rear-facing baby seat on the front passenger seat, which is protected by a frontal airbag. What must you do before setting off?

A Turn the seat to face sideways

B Deactivate the airbag

C Make sure the passenger door is locked

D Put the child in an adult seat belt

Question 35 *

You're about to reverse out of a supermarket parking bay. What do you need to be particularly aware of?

A Shopping trolleys

B Bollards and barriers

C Small children

D Other drivers

Question 36

Daytime visibility is poor and misty but not seriously reduced. Which lights should you switch on?

A Main beam headlights

B Front fog lights

C Dipped headlights

D Rear fog lights

Answers

Question 34

B - It's illegal to fit a rear-facing baby seat into a passenger seat protected by an active frontal airbag. If the airbag activates, it could cause serious injury or even death to the child. You must secure it in a different seat or deactivate the relevant airbag. Follow the manufacturer's advice when fitting a baby seat.

Question 35

C - Small children can be difficult to see when you're reversing especially if they are close to the rear of your car. Always look around thoroughly and constantly and NEVER rely on mirrors alone.

Question 36

C - Only use your fog lights when visibility is seriously reduced. Use dipped headlights in poor conditions because this helps other road users to see you without the risk of causing dazzle.

Question 37

Where would you see a contraflow bus and cycle lane?

A   On a dual carriageway

B   On a roundabout

C   On an urban motorway

D   On a one-way street

Question 38

What does this sign mean?

A   Danger ahead

B   Tunnel ahead

C   Slippery road

D   Flood water

Answers

Question 37

D - The traffic permitted to use a contraflow lane travels in the opposite direction to traffic in the other lanes on the road.

Question 38

A - This sign is shown when there is some kind of danger ahead. It may be shown on its own as a general warning for caution; or it may be shown with an information plate below describing the nature of the hazard.

Question 39

You've stalled in the middle of a level crossing and can't restart the engine. The warning bells start to ring. What should you do?

A   Run down the track to warn the signal operator

B   Get out of the car and clear of the crossing

C   Carry on trying to restart the engine

D   Push the vehicle clear of the crossing

Question 40

You're in collision with another moving vehicle. Someone is injured and your vehicle is damaged. What information should you find out?

A   Whether the other driver is licensed to drive

B   The other driver's name, address and telephone number

C   The destination of the other driver

D   The occupation of the other driver

Question 41

You're planning a long journey. Do you need to plan rest stops?

A   Yes, you should plan to stop every half an hour

B   No, you'll be less tired if you get there as soon as possible

C   Yes, regular stops help concentration

D   Yes, but only in very bad weather conditions

Answers

Question 39

B - Try to stay calm, especially if you have passengers with you. If you can't restart your engine before the warning bells ring, leave the vehicle and get yourself and any passengers well clear of the crossing. Use the phone if there is one to alert the signal operator of the danger.

Question 40

B - Try to keep calm and don't rush. Make sure that you've shared all the relevant details with the other driver before you leave the scene. If possible, take pictures and note the positions of all the vehicles involved.

Question 41

C - Try to plan your journey so that you can take rest stops. It's recommended that you take a break of at least 15 minutes after every two hours of driving or riding. This should help to maintain your concentration.

Question 42 *

You're about to join a motorway, what should you do on the approach?

A   Use the hard shoulder to build up speed

B   Give way to traffic already on the motorway

C   Only accelerate when you reach the end of the slip road

D   Slow down or stop to take proper observation

Question 43

Traffic officers operate on motorways and some primary routes in England. What are they authorised to do?

A   Stop and arrest drivers who break the law

B   Repair broken-down vehicles on the motorway

C   Stop and direct anyone on a motorway

D   Issue fixed penalty notices

Question 44

In which of these situations should you avoid overtaking?

A   Approaching a dip in the road

B   Just after a bend

C   In a one-way street

D   On a 30 mph road

Answers

Question 42

B - You should give way to traffic already on the motorway. Where possible, traffic may move over to let you in, but don't force your way into the traffic stream. Traffic could be travelling at high speed, so try to match your speed to filter in without affecting the traffic flow.

Question 43

C - Traffic officers don't have enforcement powers but are able to stop and direct people on motorways and some 'A' class roads. They only operate in England and work in partnership with the police at incidents, providing a highly trained and visible service. They're recognised by an orange-and-yellow jacket and their vehicle has yellow-and-black markings.

Question 44

A - Oncoming vehicles or other hazards can be hidden from view by dips in the road. If you can't see into the dip, wait until you have a clear view and can see that it's safe before starting to overtake.

Question 45 *

Which of these does not have authorisation to signal drivers to stop?

A   A council refuse collector

B   A police officer

C   A traffic warden

D   A school crossing patrol

Question 46

An injured person has been placed in the recovery position. They're unconscious but breathing normally. What else should be done?

A   Check their airway remains open

B   Press firmly between their shoulders

C   Place their arms by their side

D   Turn them over every few minutes

Question 47

You're driving in falling snow. What should you do if your wipers aren't clearing the windscreen?

A   Set the windscreen demister to cool

B   Use the windscreen washers

C   Partly open the front windows

D   Be prepared to clear the windscreen by hand

Answers

Question 45

A - You must obey signals to stop given by police and traffic officers, traffic wardens and school crossing patrols. Failure to do so is an offence and could lead to prosecution.

Question 46

A - After a casualty has been placed in the recovery position, make sure their airway remains open and monitor their condition until medical help arrives. Where possible, don't move a casualty unless there's further danger.

Question 47

D - Before you set off, you should make sure that you can see clearly through all the windows. Don't just rely on the wipers, as this will leave dangerous blind spots. If you need to, pull up safely and clear the windows by hand.

Question 48

Where should the head restraint be positioned for it to be most effective?

A   At least as high as the shoulders

B   At least as high as the eyes or top of the ears

C   In the lowest position and pointing forwards

D   In the highest position and tilted backwards

Question 49

How is using a hands-free phone likely to affect your driving?

A   It will divert your attention

B   It will improve your safety

C   It will improve your concentration

D   It will reduce your view

Answers

Question 48

B - An incorrectly adjusted head restraint will offer reduced protection against whiplash injury. When adjusting the head restraint, set it so that it's at least as high as the eyes or top of the ears.

Question 49

A - While you're using a phone, your attention will be divided between the call and the road. This means you're unable to take in all that's happening around your vehicle. You need to be concentrating on your driving all of the time, and especially when dealing with a hazard.

Question 50

What does this sign mean?

A   Vehicles may park on the right-hand side of the road only

B   Vehicles may park fully on the verge or footway

C   Vehicles may not park on the verge or footway

D   Vehicles may park on the left-hand side of the road only

Answers

Question 50

B - In order to keep roads free from parked cars, there are some areas where you're allowed to park on the verge. Only do this where you see the sign. Parking on verges or footways anywhere else could lead to a fine.

Need More Practise?

Become a member with UK Driving Skills and get access to around 800+ Theory Test Revision Questions, produced under licence from the DVSA.

Our interactive online tests each have 50 questions and are timed just like the real thing. You'll also be given a score at the end, plus an explanation of the answers.

Hazard Perception

We also offer packages which allow you to study for the hazard perception test with access to over 130 official practise videos.

Visit https://www.ukdrivingskills.co.uk for more info

Car 1

#36. What should you do when you see this sign at a crossroads?

- Maintain the same speed
- Carry on with great care
- Find another route
- Telephone the police

NEXT

Edit

Printed in Great Britain
by Amazon

11992032R00132